Reframing Mental Illness
ⱭꙦ

Reframing Mental Illness
CRXBO

Susan Thrasher

ISBN-13: 978-1500667528
ISBN-10: 1500667528

Contents

Introduction
CRISO

Food for thought...

According to a recent analysis of US pharmacy data, around 15% of men and 26% of women in the United States were taking some form of psychiatric medication in 2010. That's roughly one in five. In the child and adolescent population, some 7% of boys and 5% of girls were prescribed psychiatric medication, and some 15% of nursing home residents had Medicare claims for antipsychotic drugs. Overall, the psychiatric drug market in the US grew by around 22% over the ten year period from 2001 to 2010.[1]

Just stop and think about those amazing figures for a minute.

Fortune 500 lists the most profitable industries in 2012, and pharmaceuticals ranked third, after—but not far off from—network communication equipment (ranked first) and internet services (ranked second).[2]

Selling prescription drugs is clearly a very big business, and although cancer medications, respiratory agents and statin drugs earn pharmaceutical companies and their shareholders greater profits,[3] psychiatric medications play a significant role in company earnings. The US may—or may not—lead the world in the use of psychiatric drugs, but in general, psychiatric drug use in the developed world has reached mind-blowing levels—bad pun intended—and continues to climb.

Ironically, our overall mental wellness has not improved with this increased drug use. In his book *Anatomy of an Epidemic*, Robert Whitaker observed some 355,000 individuals were hospitalized with a psychiatric diagnosis in 1955 in the US. By 1987, the year the US Food and Drug Administration approved Prozac (fluoxetine) for the treatment of depression, there were some 1.25 million people receiving disability payments for mental disablement, and by 2007, that number had increased to 3.97 million, with over half a million children having been added to the roll.

Obviously, there is a difference between being hospitalized for psychiatric illness in 1955 and being on a disability roll in 2007 (but not hospitalized, that method of treatment having pretty much gone by the wayside for the majority of patients), but an 11-fold increase in officially-acknowledged psychiatric disablement begs the question: Why, given the supposed miracles of modern medical science and psychiatric medication, should the numbers of mentally disabled patients continue to rise so astronomically?

There are, of course, many possible answers to this question. It is clearly a complex issue, but here are some possibilities to consider:

- We are more aware of mental illness today.
- We are diagnosing and treating a greater range of conditions that in previous times or in other places would have been considered normal.
- Our ability to recognize and diagnose psychiatric illness has increased.
- The stigma that can come with a psychiatric diagnosis is not so much a deterrent as it once was, so more people seek help.
- Treatment for mental illness is easier and cheaper than it used to be.

- We have come to believe that mental illness is a physical problem that can best be fixed with medical solutions.
- Our lives are more complex and stressful than they used to be, resulting in a greater need for psychiatric support.
- Mental illness is now perceived as a chronic disease rather than an episodic one, hence long-term treatment is called for, and people stay on drugs longer, often for a lifetime.
- The drugs don't work.
- The medications we are being prescribed are actually making us worse, not better.

To understand where we are, it is useful to understand how we got here, and why. I think it is insightful to back up the truck and take a brief journey through history to see how the mentally ill have been cared for in the past, how some of our ideas of mental illness and treatment developed, and how all of that has evolved to create modern psychiatry and mental health care. That's what the first part of this book is about.

In the second part of this book, we'll explore ways of looking at mental "dis-ease" (lexiconically speaking, "without ease") as a non-medical condition, and examine how some people have been able to move beyond uncomfortable or distressing mental mindsets to discover empowerment, freedom, peace, joy, and ultimately, sometimes, themselves.

The title of the book is *Reframing Mental Illness*. The concept of framing—a word sometimes used to describe the context in which our thoughts and beliefs about something are formed, established, and contained—is an integral part of this process. Understanding how and why we have put—or have been led to put—a particular "frame" around some topic or issue is powerful. Learning that it is only a "frame," and that we can change that frame is even more powerful. In reframing, we give ourselves the opportunity to change the frame to give ourselves a greater range of choices and options, enabling us to take different actions should we chose to do so.

But before launching into that story...

A few words on the references in this book

Deciding how to format a book is a more complex process than it might at first seem, and this is especially true when writing includes numerous references.

Much of the first part of this book germinated from my master's thesis on antidepressants, and being a piece of scientific writing, it was full of scientific journal references and jargon. The bulk of scientific writing hangs on proving that what you are discovering is built on the firm foundation of respected researchers and writers who have gone before you, and that your work supports their work. To make that clear, the foundation needs to be well and appropriately documented.

On the other hand, I write a blog (www.susan-thrasher.blogspot.co.nz) which is written in a much more informal style, even though a fair bit of the material is referenced and often footnoted. I much prefer writing and sharing information in this less formal way rather than in a "proper" scientific format. This book bounces back a forth a bit between more formal scientific references, and more casual footnotes and links, and sometimes I've simply incorporated the references into the text. If that inconsistency bothers you, please forgive.

Modern technology also means that a great deal of interesting material is easily sourced online, making web addresses and links more useful in many cases than traditional detailed journal and book references. Unfortunately, web addresses don't format easily onto book pages because they don't "break" into words. So please forgive if they look a bit "mucky" or if one reference looks like a proper bibliography entry while another is just a web link, perhaps with a comment.

I have tried to provide these references and links for those who want to know more in whatever way seemed to work best at the time. I cannot, of course, guarantee that all of the web links will continue to be valid into an indefinite future either, or that information contained therein won't be changed, amended, or updated. I think this constant reformation of information—unlike what you get with a printed hard copy—is simply a sign of our times.

And a disclaimer

Although I have a degree in psychology, I do not have a medical background. The material presented here in no way implies any particular suggestion or recommendation for treatment or health care. You should do your own research and consult your doctor or health care practitioner prior to making any health care decisions or choices.

This is your last chance. After this, there is no turning back. You take the blue pill—the story ends, you wake up in your bed and believe whatever you want to believe. You take the red pill—you stay in Wonderland, and I show you how deep the rabbit hole goes.

--Morpheus to Neo in the movie *The Matrix*

Part I

ᘓᘔᘍᘖ

A Brief History of the Treatment Of the Mentally Ill

Chapter 1: Lunatics

Centuries ago in Europe, mental illness was ascribed to a variety of causes. Possession by evil spirits or demons was assumed to account for some cases, while others were thought to be the result of physical injuries such as a blow to the head, a response to a severe emotional shock, or the malfunctioning of physical organs throwing the body's humours—black bile, yellow bile, phlegm, and blood—out of balance.

Most of the mentally ill were cared for at home, ministered with herbal potions, prayer, and whatever distractions in the way of tasty foods, music, and company might be available. Those individuals believed possessed of demons were often exorcised by the local priest and, if that did not work, were often purged[4]—through induced vomiting, bleeding, or sweating—or punished in an attempt to drive the demons from their body.

Some people believed that mental illness could be caused by unusual sensitivity to the moon's waxing and waning. From that belief evolved the word lunatic, from the Latin words *luna*, meaning moon, and *lunaticus*, meaning moonstruck. From this word we also get the lunatic asylum.

Bedlam

During the late Middle Ages, the Renaissance, and beginnings of the industrial revolution in Europe, people suffering from mental illness who could not be cared for at home were sometimes confined to lunatic asylums. The oldest of these still in operation, and probably the most famous, is Bethlem Royal Hospital in London, founded during the reign of Henry III in 1247 as a priory or monastery. The first written records of mentally incapacitated residents present at Bethlem come from 1403, but the priory may have taken in mentally disabled individuals earlier than this. Over time, the word "bedlam"—derived from the name of this establishment—became synonymous with the general concepts of madness, uproar, and confusion.

Asylum treatment in those early times was, by modern standards, nothing short of brutal. Rooms were often dark, damp, and bitterly cold, food limited, and difficult patients were often chained to the walls with only rags to sleep on. Treatments included bleeding, blistering, and purging, as might also be done with patients suffering from physical illnesses at that time. It is probable that many impoverished individuals unable to function in normal society, as well as those seen as threatening (in whatever way) to good citizens everywhere, were often held in such places so they could be separated from the general public for the purposes of society's comfort and safety more so than for their own welfare.

Unlike modern psychiatric hospitals, Bethlem was open to the public for viewing of the patients on holidays, a popular entertainment for Londoners and visitors alike. London tourist César de Saussure described his visit to Bethlem in 1725 in a letter to his family:

> *...you find yourself in a wide and long gallery, on either side of which are a large number of little cells where lunatics of every description are shut up, and you can get a sight of these poor creatures, little windows being let into the doors.*

Many inoffensive madmen walk in the big gallery. On the second floor is a corridor and cells like those on the first floor, and this is the part reserved for dangerous maniacs, most of them being chained and terrible to behold. On holidays, numerous persons of both sexes, but belonging generally to the lower classes, visit this hospital and amuse themselves watching these unfortunate wretches, who often give them cause for laughter. On leaving this melancholy abode, you are expected by the porter to give him a penny.[5]

Reforms

Attitudes began to change in the 1800s with a variety of reforms. Morality movements in Europe and the United States brought more funding, better conditions, less restraint with iron and chains, and the building of new asylums and hospitals for the mentally ill.

One of the early reformers was the German physician Johann Christian Reil who invented the term *psychiatry* in 1808 by uniting the Greek words *psyche* (soul) and *iatry* (physician, from the Greek *iatros*). Reil argued that the study and treatment of the human psyche should have the same medical standing as the other main branches of medicine, surgery and pharmacology. He believed that mental illness developed from the fragmentation of self, an incomplete or poorly-formed personality, an inability to separate self from non-self, and/or was a reflection of one's wider social conditions. He argued for more humane and caring hospital treatment for the mentally ill, advocating normal and pleasant surroundings, a good diet, regular exercise, dancing, books and other mental diversions, music "to quiet the storm of the soul," a little opium to be mixed into the patient's wine, and more traditional (for the time) physical treatments like cold baths and the application of hot wax.[6]

The title "father of American psychiatry" is often given to Dr Benjamin Rush, who served as a doctor on the staff of the Pennsylvania Hospital from 1783 until his death in 1813. Rush campaigned for state funding to pay for a separate ward for the insane so patients could be provided with decent beds and adequate food and would be encouraged to engage in conversation, a variety of activities, and music. Rush believed that mental illness was a disease of the mind, not a product of demonic possession, moral failure or moon madness.

Treatment-wise, however, Rush advocated a variety of physical interventions to tame the patient's madness including bleeding—"as much as four-fifths of the blood in the body"—blistering, and purging, and he invented a sensory-deprivation device called the tranquillizing chair into which patients could be strapped for many hours on end with their vision restricted by a large headpiece, as well as a spinning board, designed to render a patient so weak and dizzy that any wild thoughts might be simply driven from his brain. He published the first American textbook on psychiatry, *Medical Inquiries and Observations Upon the Diseases of the Mind* in 1812.

Early in the 1800s the Quakers established several mental health retreats in America based on a gentler approach to curing madness that came to be known as "moral treatment". At the Vermont asylum founded in 1834, for example, accommodation for the mentally ill was in furnished bedrooms (rather than cells or hospital wards), and the establishment incorporated a chapel, a gymnasium, discussion groups, patient outings, and a variety of patient-managed enterprises. The emphasis was on meaningful work, fresh air, healthy food, mind-enriching diversions, and a supportive staff for patient recovery, without the use of torturous physical interventions like bleeding, purging, spinning, or the ice water baths that were in common use elsewhere.

A later example, the Athens Hospital for the Insane in Athens, Ohio, first opened its doors in 1874, and remained in operation until 1993. In the earlier years, this large establishment operated as an almost self-sufficient community with fields, gardens, livestock, a dairy, a laundry, a steam plant, and even a carriage house. Much of the daily work was carried out by patients, who were encouraged to engage in ordinary activities to ensure their lives were as normal as possible.

Cure rates at these moral asylums were better than 50%, in some cases as high as 80%, but they were generally only available for those who could afford such gentle and comfortable treatment. Early records show the most common causes for admission for men were masturbation, alcoholism (intemperance), and fever, while post-partum depression, menstrual problems, and problems with menopause accounted for the majority of female patients. Epilepsy, another frequent cause for admission, was common to both sexes.

It may be evident from this that a wide variety of "conditions" fell under the umbrella of mental illness prior to the 20th century. Any misunderstood or socially-inappropriate behaviours from epileptic fits to masturbation, from hysteria to alcoholism to post-menopausal mood changes could be interpreted as a sign of insanity, resulting in asylum incarceration and/or a variety of treatments ranging from bleeding and purging to spinning tables and psychoanalysis.

Originally built to house 570 patients (twice the number considered an appropriate maximum size), by the 1950s the Athens Hospital was housing over 1800 patients. And part of the reason for that increase in size to the point of overcrowding—common in mental institutions across the US—was due to the sincere and well-meant efforts of individuals like Dorothea Dix.

Dix, an American social activist in the mid-1800s, wanted to see moral treatment made available even to those without the economic means to pay for it. She campaigned successfully in many states and before Congress over a 40-year period for bigger budgets, more land, and improved care for the mentally disabled, as well as for the blind, the deaf, and prisoners.

The downside of her activist work is that while access to more humane care became easier and cheaper, public institutions reflected tighter budgets by growing larger whilst keeping staff numbers reasonably low (and low-paid) and cutting out 'luxuries' like chapels, gymnasiums, and expensive recreational activities.

The loss of a warm, community feeling coupled with poorer staff to patient ratios and less-educated staff also led to an increased use of restraint with difficult patients. Not surprisingly, recovery rates declined. By the 1930s, the recovery and discharge rate from mental hospitals had dropped to about 15%.

Mental illness as a medical condition

The post-Civil War period in America saw the rise of many asylums across the US, along with a significant change in how American insane asylums were run. Where before, many moral asylums functioned without medical guidance, it became compulsory to have a doctor on the staff by the mid-1800s. Many doctors, fresh from the bloody field hospitals of the Civil War, called themselves neurologists and sought civilian employment in mental asylums. Physical and medical treatments for the mentally ill were now back on the cards, including the use of drugs like opium and morphine to sedate patients, and the use of straitjackets, an old French invention considered kinder than chains, to control them.

In Europe, meanwhile, German psychiatrist Emil Kraepelin argued that mental illness occurred as a result of physical and/or genetic abnormalities that could be understood, classified, and diagnosed just like any other diseases. In his textbook on psychiatry, first published in Germany in 1883 and revised regularly (English translations were made available in 1902 and 1907) as the *Compendium der Psychiatrie*, Kraepelin endeavoured to identify and classify the clusters and patterns of symptoms typical of the psychiatric disorders that he identified in his work.

Kraepelin paid particular attention to the state of psychosis, an abnormal condition of the mind where the subject appears to have lost contact with reality. Kraepelin believed there were two main types of psychosis: the range of mood disorders on the continuum between melancholia (what we now call depression) and mania, and *dementia praecox* (what we now call schizophrenia). Although the same symptoms could occur in either type of psychosis, Kraepelin believed the symptoms' origins were different, and that particular patterns of thought and behaviour occurred in one type of psychosis or the other.

According to Kraepelin, melancholia and mania and the other conditions that occurred in the mood/emotion continuum generally manifested as periodic illnesses that interrupted periods of normal health. He believed this spectrum of disorders originated outside the body, were not life-long conditions, were treatable, and that a complete recovery was not only possible but likely.

He thought d*ementia praecox*, on the other hand, was caused by organic changes to the brain, was basically degenerative, and could not be cured. He identified three types of *dementia praecox*: catatonia (when movement becomes stiff, stilted, or non-existent); hebephrenia (inappropriate emotions or actions); and paranoia (delusions of persecution or grandeur).

In retrospect, it seems likely that many of Kraepelin's dementia praecox patients were actually suffering from the [possibly viral] brain disease encephalitis lethargica, which was not identified as a disease until 1917 when it reached epidemic proportions in Europe, and which has a poor prognosis for recovery[7]. The symptoms of catatonia, muscular weakness, delayed mental and physical responses, and abnormal movements or tics identified by Kraepelin as indicators of *dementia praecox* are also symptoms of encephalitis lethargic.

Kraepelin's descriptions and his classification of mental disorders, however, was the first to be readily accessible to anyone working within the profession. His work was widely used by psychiatrists in the early part of the 20th century, especially in Europe.

In the US, however, the interest was more in statistical classification: seven categories of mental illness were identified in the 1880 US census: melancholia, mania, monomania (partial insanity whereby the patient appears normal in most ways but demonstrates some abnormal quirk or obsessive idea), paresis (partial paralysis), dementia, dipsomania (alcoholism), and epilepsy.

Early 20th century treatments

Although spinning boards and chairs, extensive bleeding and purging, and ice water baths had more-or-less been left behind by 1900, a variety of new "scientific" and medical procedures for restless and distressed psychiatric patients took their place. In his book *Mad in America: Bad Science, Bad Medicine, and the Enduring Mistreatment of the Mentally Ill,* Robert Whitaker presents a profile of the various treatments popular during this time, and I briefly summarize some of them in this and the following two sections. I highly recommend the book for any readers interested in learning more about the history of psychiatric treatment.

Most psychiatric hospitals incorporated some form of hydrotherapy in their patient treatment repertoire in the early 20th century. These included the soaking of patients, often restrained, in hot, warm or cold baths for hours or even days at a time; the use of "needle" showers of pressurized cold water; and the wrapping of patients in wet sheets that, while seriously uncomfortable when wet, became torturous as the cotton sheets dried and shrank to create a vice-like sensation.[8]

Gynecological operations were performed on as many as 50% of female mental patients between 1890 and 1910, most commonly hysterectomies (removal of the uterus) and removal of the ovaries. For several years, tooth extraction became popular with the belief that mental illness might be associated with mouth infections. Other mental patients had their tonsils, gall bladders, or appendices removed in an attempt to tame their madness.

Deep sleep therapy, popular in the early 1900s, involved using barbiturate drugs to induce a coma in the patient and keeping him/her unconscious for days on end. In spite of claims of miraculous cures with this treatment, a 6% mortality rate saw it disappear over time.

Another treatment involved injecting patients with malaria to create a malarial infection and fever. Developed by Austrian psychiatrist Julius Wagner-Jauregg, who won a Nobel Prize in Medicine for the discovery of this treatment in 1927, it produced a cure rate over 25% for patients experiencing psychiatric paralysis, especially (ironically) if they concurrently suffered from syphilis. Unfortunately, weaker paralytic patients often succumbed to the malarial fever itself and died.[9]

When refrigeration therapy, which involved packing the patient's body in ice and dropping his/her body temperature by 5-10° C, was tried on 16 patients, three of them died. It was not used again.

In the 1930s, insulin-coma therapy became so popular, the *Reader's Digest* called it a "bedside miracle," especially for schizophrenic patients. This therapy involved giving the patient injections of insulin to lower blood sugar levels to the point where s/he passed out and the brain would begin to haemorrhage. The patient would then be revived. Patients often underwent daily insulin coma treatment for a month or more. The belief was that the haemorrhages destroyed diseased brain tissue.

Following treatment, patients were reported to be more childlike and co-operative. Mortality rates from the procedure were about 5%, and the process was resource intensive and expensive to administer, but in spite of this, insulin-coma therapy remained in use until the 1950s.

There was a significant concept emerging here: that severe stress or trauma to the body or brain could trigger—at least for a time—relief from disturbing mental symptoms, although whether that relief was more for the patient's benefit or more for the caregivers is less clear.

Induced seizures

Another common treatment between 1935 and 1941, especially for patients diagnosed as manic-depressive (today called bipolar), was the administration of the drug metrazol, a circulatory and respiratory stimulant, in sufficient doses to generate convulsions severe enough to fracture bones and loosen teeth. Like insulin-coma therapy, metrazol therapy was often administered as multiple doses over several days or weeks. Following initial "improvement" rates—characterized, as with insulin-coma therapy, as patients becoming more docile, childlike, friendly, and co-operative—after a time, patients usually relapsed into chronic depression.

A "better" method for inducing convulsions in mental patients was pioneered in the 1940s and 1950s and was called Electro-Convulsive Therapy, or ECT, where electric currents were passed through the brain to produce seizures. Although acknowledged as causing memory loss and an overall lowering of intellect, the belief at the time was summed up by advocate Harry Stack Sullivan who remarked, "It is better to be a contented imbecile than a schizophrenic."

As with insulin coma and metrazol therapy, multiple sessions were common, and with the co-administration of paralyzing drugs, the risk of bone fractures was minimized. Remission rates with ECT vary between 30 and 80%.[10] Although no longer commonly used today, ECT, also called electro-shock treatment, remains a treatment option for patients suffering from severe depression who have been unresponsive to other forms of treatment.

The lobotomy

The 1930s also saw the introduction of the lobotomy (or leucotomy), a surgical procedure which earned Portuguese neurologist Antonio Egas Moniz a Nobel Prize in 1949, although he had developed and first begun using the procedure on patients as early as 1936. Essentially a severing of the connections to and from the prefrontal cortex of the brain, it was initially performed by drilling holes in the skull, inserting an ice-pick sort of instrument, and wiggling it around a bit to destroy the cellular connections.

American Walter Freeman perfected a method of inserting the pick through the eye sockets, making the operation so simple he was able to hit the road in his camper van (he called it his "lobotomobile") and travel around the US to various mental hospitals in the 1940s, taking just 20 minutes to perform each surgery.

A lobotomy did not necessarily make patients well, and it often resulted in unexpected personality changes, but it usually created a level of pacification by reducing emotional responses and increasing apathy without causing major impairment of intelligence or motor function, thus rendering more violent, emotional, or difficult patients biddable while allowing them to retain basic functionality. However, it was not always a successful operation.

One of the more infamous "failures" of the lobotomy procedure was Rosemary Kennedy, the sister of John F. Kennedy, who underwent the surgery at the age of 23 for "moodiness" and was left with the mental capacity of a young child. She spent the rest of her life institutionalized.

Around 40,000 lobotomies were performed in the US, 17,000 in the UK, and smaller numbers elsewhere before the practice fell out of fashion in the 1970s.

Chapter 2: Drug Treatment Before 1950
CBEO

A variety of substances have been used for centuries to modulate and modify moods, but until the mid-1900s, few drugs were included as part of a mental patient's treatment in the hospital setting except as purges (to induce vomiting or evacuation of the bowels or both) or as a way to sedate patients for easier handling by their caregivers.

Early and well-recognized mood modifiers included alcohol, cannabis, opium, and a variety of herbal potions and teas. Laudanum, made as a tincture of alcohol and opium poppy along with various herbs and other flavourings, has been around since the 1500s and was widely available until the early 20th century. It was used for pain, colds, coughs, fevers, and diarrhoea, but not specifically as a treatment for mental distress. Like opiates in general, it is highly addictive.

Psychiatric drug treatment in the 1800s

Morphine, derived from the latex sap that oozes from an opium poppy seedpod, is a more powerful painkiller than laudanum. It was first extracted and prepared in the early 1800s, and was first sold commercially by the small German apothecary shop Merck (the origin of the modern pharmaceutical giant of the same name) in 1827. Another opium derivative, codeine, appeared in 1832. Less powerful that morphine, it was used for less intense pain and coughs. Both substances are addictive.

With the advent of the Age of Science, new chemical compounds were discovered and became available for treatment for the psychiatrically distressed. Potassium bromide, a sedative and hypnotic (causes sleep), first appeared in 1826 as a treatment for epilepsy, nervous disorders, and to lessen sexual urges. It was the first effective anti-epileptic drug, although the nausea and vomiting that occur after administration, and it's propensity to cause dependence, mean it is rarely used today.

Chloral hydrate was discovered in 1832 and was also used as a sedative and sleeping agent. It remained popular through most of the 19th century along with paraldehyde, first synthesized in 1829 for use as an industrial resin and solvent. Paraldehyde's anti-convulsant and sedative properties were discovered in the later 1800s, and its relatively good safety record made it a popular choice for treatment of hospitalized psychotic and epileptic patients up through the 1960s.

Lithium

In the 1800s, an era when "taking the waters" for health was popular, lithium salts—present in small quantities in many natural mineral waters—became popular as a tonic for easement of gout and rheumatism, conditions believed to be caused by concentrations of uric acid. By the late 1800s, a few doctors also began giving it to patients for depression and mania. By the early 1940s however, following numerous cases of poisoning and several deaths, the use of lithium salts for any conditions had virtually disappeared, and the US Food and Drug Administration (FDA) banned the use of lithium in 1949[11].

However, also in 1949, Australian John Cade published a paper[12] in which he cited the results of administration of lithium carbonate to ten psychiatric patients experiencing mania, six diagnosed with *dementia praecox*—the term schizophrenia was first introduced by the Swiss psychiatrist Eugen Bleuler in 1908, but it took some time for it to become the preferred term—and three melancholic (depressed) patients.

Cade considered lithium carbonate a preferable drug choice—provided doses were kept small—to the more-commonly-used bromides and paraldehyde because although it caused sedation, it did not cause sleepiness. Most of the manic and schizophrenic patients in his study were reported as being transformed from "noisy, restless, and aggressive" to "settling down," "distinctly quieter," and "practically normal," while the depressed patients experienced "no improvement, but neither was there any aggravation of the depression."[13]

Clearly, this was a useful drug for management of difficult patients within a hospital setting. It would be some decades, however, before the use of lithium for mania and bipolar disorder (manic-depression) would become more widespread.

What wasn't reported in Cade's study was the later death of one patient from lithium toxicity, and toxic effects experienced by others; Cade later gave up on the use of lithium with his patients.[14]

Patent medicines

One of the problems with these drugs and substances from a commercial standpoint is that anyone could make them. Being able to claim ownership for a medicine and therefore being able to market and charge for it whatever customers were willing to pay would clearly give a distinct financial advantage to the owner/seller. The patent idea first appeared in Europe as early as the 1400s and signified exclusive rights to market a particular item by royal or governmental decree.

In the 1800s, "patent medicines" became very popular with the general public. These referred to branded compounds and a variety of pills and tonics ranging from John Hooper's Female Pills (with "anti-hysterik ingredients") to Kickapoo Indian Sagwa ("the only remedy Indians ever use") to Stanley's Snake Oil (a liniment "good for man or beast"). Advertisements for these products in the press increased revenue for a burgeoning media industry, ensured a good turnover for patent owners and producers, and increased customer sales for those who stocked the products on their shop shelves. Many of these patent-medicine potions were based on alcohol and/or opium-derived compounds and few carried "official" government patents. At that time in the US there were no government regulations on potion ingredients or what results could be claimed about health products.

That changed in 1906 in the US when Congress passed the Pure Food and Drug Act, essentially a "truth in labelling" law that required any "dangerous" ingredients be cited on the product label. Alcohol, morphine, opium and cannabis were all on the government's "danger" list.

By 1912, an amendment had been added to the act forbidding "false and fraudulent" claims about a product. A new government regulatory body, the US department of Food, Drugs, and Insecticides, came into being in 1927, and that was transmuted into the US Food and Drug Administration (US FDA) in 1930.

In 1938 the US government passed a new law specifying that any new drugs would have to be reviewed for product safety, and identified certain drugs as appropriate for use only under medical supervision, although the category of "prescription only" did not officially come into law in the US until 1951.

Chemistry comes of age

The first trade-marketed anxiolytic (anti-anxiety medication) from a chemistry lab was the barbiturate barbitol, synthesized by German chemists in 1903 and marketed by Bayer in 1904 under the trade name *Veronal*. This was followed by phenobarbital (Luminal) in 1912 and anobarbital in 1923.[15] These were used in mental hospitals for the deep sleep therapy mentioned earlier. Over a thousand barbiturate compounds were synthesized, and about 50 were brought to the market, but significant issues with toxicity and dependence made the need for safer sedative formulations apparent.

In 1929, Gordon Alles, a biochemist working on decongestants, developed a new compound, beta-phenyl-isopropylamine, which came to be known later as amphetamine. A base form of the compound was patented by the pharmaceutical company Smith, Kline and French (SKF) in 1933, and the Benzadrine Inhaler—"a volatile vasoconstrictor" according to a 1943 SKF advertisement--became "an official item of issue"[16] in the US Army Air Forces during World War II. In addition, it was sold over the counter to civilians for more than a decade.

SKF soon found other uses for the new drug, which stimulated the central nervous system, and in 1937 they received the American Medical Association (AMA) seal of approval for a tablet-form of amphetamine called Benzedrine Sulfate for use in the treatment of narcolepsy, Parkinsonism, and minor depression.[17] SKF recruited a champion for Benzedrine Sulfate in Harvard neurologist and psychiatrist Abraham Myerson, author of the then-popular book *When Life Loses its Zest*. Myerson reasoned that since depression is expressed by a lack of energy, enthusiasm and focus (he liked to use the then-obscure nineteenth-century term *anhedonia*, which means "lack of pleasure"), and amphetamine is a stimulant, amphetamine would be a perfect antidote to elevate the depressed patient's mood. SKF used Myerson's reputation, medical background, and logical reasoning to launch an advertising campaign for the new drug aimed at general practitioners.[18]

Full page advertisements for SKF's Benzedrine Sulphate appeared in medical journals in the 1940s promising "a non-narcotic drug capable of alleviating depression", patients having "a sense of increased energy, mental alertness, and capacity for work," and "immediate results, in some instances spectacular." Doctors were prompted to recommend the product to their patients, a savvy marketing move on SKF's part given the trust patients place in their doctor's advice. Sales doubled in the first year of advertising.

After the end of World War II in 1945, mental illness became a huge issue for many nations as returning veterans faced the emotional struggles inherent with their return to civilian life. (Today we call this PTSD—Post Traumatic Stress Disorder). Mental hospitals filled to bursting.

In 1946, the US Congress passed a National Mental Health Act promising economic support for research into the prevention, diagnosis, and treatment of mental illness, followed by the establishment of the National Institute of Mental Health (NIMH) in 1949. What the country needed, most thought, was modern medical solutions to solve the problems of the mentally ill.

It was the beginning of the modern age of drug treatment for mental illness. Interesting, exciting and profitable times were ahead for pharmaceutical companies. But before we carry on with that story, let us look briefly at a different historical track regarding the treatment of the mentally ill.

Chapter 3: Hypnosis and Psychoanalysis
ⓒ℘℘

We return to Europe in the eighteenth century where two gentlemen were achieving remarkable cures for numerous distressing conditions without hospitalization or long-term treatment.

Exorcism

In 1774, Joseph Gassner, an Austrian Catholic priest, published a booklet explaining his theory that there are two kinds of disease: physical ones for which a physician is the most appropriate healer, and illnesses caused by the possession of devils or spirits. After asking his patients to put their faith in Jesus Christ, Gassner would entreat the devils to make themselves known. If no devil-induced symptoms appeared, the illness, he believed, was clearly physical. If, however, symptoms manifested when the devils were asked to perform, then he believed the disease was caused by possession and could be dealt with through exorcism.

A written account of one of his healings was given by an observer in 1775:

> *The first patients were two nuns who had been forced to leave their community on account of convulsive fits. Gassner told the first one to kneel before him, asked her briefly about her name, her illness, and whether she agreed than anything he would order should happen. She agreed. Gassner then pronounced solemnly in Latin: "If there be anything*

preternatural about this disease, I order in the name of Jesus that it manifest itself immediately." The patient started at once to have convulsions. According to Gassner, this was proof that the convulsions were caused by an evil spirit and not by natural illness, and he now proceeded to demonstrate that he had power over the demon, whom he ordered in Latin to produce convulsions in various parts of the patient's body; he called forth in turn the exterior manifestations of grief, silliness, scrupulosity, anger, and so on, and even the appearance of death. All his orders were punctually executed. It now seemed logical that, once a demon had been tamed to that point, it should be relatively easy to expel him, which Gassner did. He then proceeded in the same manner with the second nun. After the séance had ended, Abbé Bourgeois asked whether it had been very painful; she answered that she had only a vague memory of what had happened and that she had not suffered much. Gassner then treated a third patient, a high-born lady who had previously been afflicted with melancholia. Gassner called for the melancholia and explained to the lady what she was to do in order to overcome it in case she was troubled by it again.[19]

In spite of resounding success with many of his patients, Gassner incited controversy with his methods. At that time, Europe was moving into the age of Enlightenment, and belief in spirit possession, so popular in Europe (and parts of America) between the 1400s and the mid-to-late 1700s, was rapidly being replaced by a growing belief in scientific principles, which had little to do with things that cannot be seen or measured. Anything that seemed "superstitious" came under increasing scrutiny, and concepts such as "demon possessions," "exorcism" and "miracle cures" called for honest scepticism from the public.

Mesmer

The German/Austrian physician Franz Mesmer—from whose name we get the word *mesmerize*—came to public attention about the same time as Gassner using a similar method, but with a more "scientific" approach. He claimed to have discovered a force he called "animal magnetism" and his work with it, at least initially, involved the use of magnets.

Mesmer believed that a "subtle fluid" or energy flowed within and between people, the earth, and heavenly bodies; that disease resulted from an uneven distribution of this fluid within the body; that the flow of this fluid could be altered, channelled, and even moved from person to person; and that doing so could evoke a minor crisis states that could then be cured.

Mesmer was reportedly a man of considerable intelligence, charm and showmanship. He created scientific authority for his patients by using a variety of substances and devices including a container of magnetized water, music from magnetized instruments, and mirrors, which he said would increase the magnetic influences. His curative method then involved sitting in front of the patient and staring into the patient's eyes while pressing the patient's thumbs into his hands, moving his hands along the patient's arms, and pressing his fingers into the patient's lower chest or abdomen. Like Gassner, he believed that a "magnetizer" in rapport with his patient could bring forth symptoms in a controlled situation and enable them to be cured on the spot. By all accounts, he experienced considerable success as a healer for just about everything from epilepsy to hysteria (excessive emotionality) to haemorrhoids. It may come as no surprise that today Mesmer is often considered the father of hypnosis.

Mesmer's theory of a "subtle magnetic fluid," however, was ridiculed by commissioners of the French Academies of Science and Medicine, where his cures—which were not challenged—were attributed to "imagination" rather than sound medical practice and were thus dismissed. Disappointed in his inability to achieve scientific credibility with his theory and healings, Mesmer languished into obscurity in his later years. He died in 1815.

Hypnosis

Mesmerism did not die with Mesmer, however, but simmered in an "underground" way with some followers continuing to advocate the animal magnetism theory while others evolved a new idea that the method's success was attributable not to the flow of magnetic fluids but to the psychological properties of belief and suggestion.

In 1826, the French naturalist Joseph Philippe François Deluze and magnetist Etienne Félix d'Hénin de Cuvillers, who reportedly first used the words *hypnotisme* and *hypnotiste*, convinced the Académie de Médecine to reopen the investigation into mesmerism. Their report published in 1831 acknowledged positive health results obtainable with the method.

The British physician John Elliotson, an enthusiastic supporter of this new method, opened his London Mesmeric Infirmary in 1849 where he pioneered the use of hypnosis for anaesthesia and pain control, claiming that mesmerism was not only safer than using ether, but also more effective. The infirmary remained open for about two decades until the discovery of more popular chemical anaesthetics [than ether] such as nitrous oxide, coupled with public scepticism of "it's all in your mind so it isn't real" pain control, saw it eventually close.

Meanwhile, back in France, Jean-Martin Charcot, director of medicine at the Saltpêtrière Women's Asylum, was interested in female hysteria. According to Hippocrates who supposedly first described the condition more than 2000 years ago (hysteria comes from the Greek word *hystericus* meaning "suffering in the womb"), hysterical women were best treated by marriage and pregnancy.

Charcot believed otherwise. He theorized that hysteria, characterized by a lack of self-control and imaginary fears, actually originated as an emotional response to some traumatic event in the patient's past. He recognised a close parallel between the stages he'd identified with hysteria and the stages of hypnosis: catalepsy (a trance-like state), lethargy (a state of sluggishness or apparent indifference), and somnambulism (performing actions without conscious awareness). Charcot believed that women suffering from hysteria were particularly susceptible to hypnosis, and that hypnosis was basically an induced hysteria.

Charcot is best known today for his work as a neurologist, having been the first to describe multiple sclerosis and doing much to advance our understanding of Parkinson's disease, but his work with—and observations about—hypnosis were important.

Freud and psychoanalysis

One of Charcot's most famous students was the Austrian psychiatrist Sigmund Freud, who came to Paris on a fellowship study in 1885, and developed a particular interest in Charcot's work with hypnosis and hysteria. When he returned to Vienna, Freud began using hypnosis in his own clinical practice.

Rather than creating suggestibility with his patients to enable a clearance of problems, he altered the hypnosis technique to encourage his patients to talk freely about their symptoms and the historical origins of their symptoms in a way he called "free association". He also encouraged his patients to talk about their dreams, and the possible meanings of those dreams. His method of treatment became colloquially known as "talk therapy". By the mid-1890s, Freud had abandoned the word "hypnosis" from his treatment descriptions and had begun using a new term for the talk therapy he had invented: psychoanalysis.

Freud developed many theories about how the mind works during his career. For example, he believed that the mind has distinct parts: the conscious mind, which is where all of the "stuff" we are actively aware of *now* is kept available; the pre-conscious or sub-conscious mind which is where the recent and regularly-accessed material is stored; and the unconscious mind, which is where we store all of the "stuff" that underlies our personality but which we don't actively access under normal circumstances.

Freud believed that distressing and traumatic memories were often suppressed from the conscious mind and relegated to the unconscious mind, where they continued to influence thoughts, experiences, behaviours, and dreams without the subject being aware of that influence.

Another significant model developed by Freud involved the three parts of the *psyche* (the human mind or soul) that he called the *id*, the *ego*, and the *super-ego*. Briefly, the *id* represents the instinctual drives that push us to satisfy our bodily needs for survival, food, shelter, and sex, as well as the impetus towards pleasure and fun, and away from pain and distress. Freud's definition of *ego* refers to the rational, mostly-conscious part of the psyche that regulates the *id* through the synthesis of information, use of judgement, reality testing, and intellectual functioning: in short, common sense. Freud's *super-ego* is a sort of guiding conscience, controlling our sense of right and wrong and helping us to make socially-acceptable choices; it's the silent, unconscious voice of the father and of society itself. According to Freud, these three parts of the psyche act as checks and balances on each other, but can create conflict as well in the form of repression, rationalization, guilt, denial, compensation, and fantasy, to name a few of the defence mechanisms thus generated.

Several of Freud's theories revolved around sex and sexuality. Rising out of his repression theory, for example, was the idea of the Oedipus complex: a belief that children were unconsciously sexually attracted to their parent of the opposite sex. (In Greek mythology, Oedipus unknowingly murdered his father and married his mother to become king of Thebes.) Another example: Freud believed that dreams were highly symbolic and carried a significant sexual content. Long, slender objects in dreams he identified as phallic symbols: cigars, knives, cannons, sticks; while things that served as containers in dreams were interpreted symbolically as connected with female genitalia: bowls, caves, suitcases, pockets. Dream activities like dancing, fencing, or riding a horse were interpreted by Freud as symbolic of sexual intercourse itself.

Although Freud died in 1939, his theories and method of psychoanalysis for the treatment of mental distress, remained popular until the 1960s. The now-clichéd picture of the psychiatrist sitting in his chair behind the patient taking notes, with the patient inevitably depicted lying on a couch and talking, comes directly from Freud's method of working.

Jung and self-exploration

Freud's work influenced many other psychiatrists. One of these was the Swiss psychiatrist Carl Gustav Jung, who first began working with Freud in 1906, an association that was to last about seven years until their different perspectives on the nature of mind and consciousness caused a decisive split. Like Freud, Jung was a working therapist who believed that psychoanalysis was an important and effective way to resolving internal issues and conflicts that he believed were at the seat of mental illness.

Unlike Freud, Jung did not believe that the unconscious was a compendium of repressed thoughts and desires, or that sex was necessarily the dominant theme. Also unlike Freud, Jung worked with his patients in partnership, allowing both of them to learn about human nature together in a sort of joint-partnership. He was also very much a philosopher. He came to believe that therapy was, at its best, a process of self-exploration, and exploration of the parts of self that, when combined, create a sense of wholeness. He was interested in the meaning of life and the importance relationships play in an individual's personal development.

One significant concept that comes from Jungian psychology is the idea of the personal and collective unconscious. Most of us today understand that we have an unconscious mind that keeps us breathing without our thinking about it, ensures we can walk without thinking about how to do it, that makes us react (or not) when a ball or a bee or a bear comes towards us, and where our personal memories are stored. And we may recognize, if we think about it, that this unconscious portion of our mind is much bigger than the part of the mind that holds the things we are consciously aware of at any given time.

To clarify that idea, imagine how an iceberg has only 10-15% of the chunk of ice sitting above the sea water, and think of that visible part of the iceberg as the conscious mind. The unconscious mind is like the underwater part of the iceberg that you cannot see from the surface. Or think of your computer screen, where you may have several "active" files open, but many more plus an operating system and various programs that are not on-screen or in conscious awareness.

The concept of a collective unconscious that we all share remains a controversial belief today, but as a part of that idea, Jung postulated that there are key archetypes that we all, as human beings, instinctively understand. At the centre of these archetypes is the Self. In addition, Jung believed we all instinctively understand other archetypal roles such as the Mother, the Father, the Child, the Wise One, the Hero, and the Shadow. The Shadow—this is a Jungian term—is the stuff we don't like about ourselves. Jung believed the Shadow to be a most useful area to recognize and explore in a therapeutic sense.

Like Freud, Jung was interested in dreams, but while Freud interpreted dreams as "wish fulfilments" and ascribed specific meanings to particular items that might appear in a dream, Jung suggested that dreams are a way the unconscious can present to you what it is noticing in a personal but often metaphorical way. He believed that only the dreamer can truly know what the dream is about, not the therapist (although a good therapist, having worked with the patient for a while, might have some ideas).

While Freud might pronounce an apple in your dream as symbolic of the sexual temptation presented by Eve in the Garden of Eden, Jung would say that, to a fruit farmer at harvest time or a woman who just made apple strudel that day, an apple might be just an apple. Or it could be a metaphor for profit, or work, or satisfaction, or pride, or nature, or art or health, or sustenance, or fecundity, but that would depend entirely upon how the apple was portrayed in the dream and how the dreamer interpreted it.

Adler and individual psychology

Another of Freud's followers—for a while at least (although in later years, he vehemently denied it)— who had a huge impact on modern methods of therapy was the Austrian physician Alfred Adler, known today as the father of Individual Psychology. Adler considered himself first and foremost a community psychologist, and was the first to work with patients and their families, with a focus on family dynamics, and the first to practice group counselling—no couches here! Unlike Freud and Jung, Adler believed that individuals were goal-driven, and that family and social groups and environmental factors have at least as much effect on a person's mental health as internal processes like thoughts and beliefs. He believed that people are largely responsible for who they are, and that individuals create stories about themselves in childhood which influence their perceptions and choices as adults. An example of this would be the story "I'm not good with numbers"—perhaps based on something a child's mother or father might have often said—that then carries over into adult beliefs, behaviours, and choices.

Adler did not tell his patients what he thought their problems were, but used a Socratic method of asking questions to help his patients make their own discoveries about themselves. Alfred Adler died in 1937.

Although psychoanalysis (also sometimes called depth psychology) could be insightful and effective in helping patients overcome mental illness without any physical intervention, the process was time-consuming and expensive. Freud and Jung and their contemporaries met regularly with their patients, sometimes over many years, for one-on-one sessions. Adler's use of community, family, and group therapy made delivery somewhat more wide-spread, but it still involved a slow process of discovery, learning and healing.

A variety of psychotherapy models were developed over the next few decades, and educated clients with time, money, and the desire to do so continued to experience personal growth and understanding—and often resolution—of their mental problems through therapy.

Meanwhile, it was bringing mental illness into focus for "the masses" that drove what happened in the second half of the 20th century.

Chapter 4: Modern Psychiatric Drugs
∞

1950s—the set up

The 20th century was an era of machines. It heralded the development of the motor car, the airplane, transistor radios, air conditioning, black-n-white and then colour television sets, satellites and computers.

Human beings too were often characterized as marvellous machines, as depicted in Dr Kahn's 1949 book *The Secret of Life—The Human Machine and How it Works*, and mechanical fixes for the human body became both assumed and commonplace. Heart surgeons installed the first pace-makers, kidney dialysis allowed for a mechanical cleansing of the blood if ailing kidneys could no longer handle the job, knees and hips could be replaced with mechanical joints, and artificial limbs could permit disabled athletes to remain active, and sometimes even return to the sports they loved.

The medical assumption regarding mental illness in the 20th century was that the patient's problem was caused by some sort of mechanical malfunction in the brain. And that was a useful idea, especially if you wanted to make money, because machines can be "fixed". If your car breaks down, you take it to a mechanic and get it fixed. If your arm is broken, you take it to the doctor and get it fixed. If your brain is broken...

The 20th century was also an era of entrepreneurs and economics. We may smile now at the naivety of folks queuing up to buy Kickapoo Indian Sagwa or

John Hooper's Female Pills, and be little short of horrified at Walter Freeman travelling around the US with his lobotomobile, eager to scramble our brains with his ice pick, but drug marketing in the post World War II era capitalized on people's belief in a medical (and scientific) fix for their problems. Marketers just became more sophisticated with their techniques.

Ultimately, marketing is about recognizing an opportunity and providing products that will satisfy people's needs or desires in exchange for money. The first step for any marketer is to ask if there are folks out there wanting to buy the products, or ask if there is some new kind of product that a company could make to satisfy a particular need that they've noticed.

If a product exists and it isn't selling well, there are several strategies that can be used. The marketer can make the products more readily available, make them more appealing, increase exposure to buyers through advertising, make products easier to use, adjust the cost, and/or get trusted authorities to endorse the products.

If there isn't a product yet, but a particular need has been recognized, then it's time to create an appropriate product to fill that market niche, or adapt an existing product and present it to buyers in such a way that it seems to satisfy that particular need. Sometimes marketers start from an even more basic level: they *create* a need or desire, and then set out to satisfy the need or desire they have created.

You will remember SKF's market plumping for their amphetamine drug Benzedrine Sulfate in the 1930s and 1940s. They made their product attractive by getting approval from the AMA; they offered the product in two convenient forms, pill or inhaler; they utilized clever copywriters to play up the drug's qualities: "non-narcotic", "immediate results", "alleviate depression," "increased energy and capacity for work"; they targeted doctors who could recommend the drug to patients by running full-page advertisements in medical journals; and they got a well-known psychiatrist and author to endorse the drug. They also promoted the drug to doctors who had influence within the military, making it accessible and desirable for sale and distribution to a large number of perfectly healthy customers who needed to stay alert, and in doing so, opened up a significant and valuable new drug market (and way of looking at psychiatric drugs).

The role and importance of doctors in drug sales increased in significance in the US in 1952 with the Durham-Humphrey Amendment. This law change mandated that some drugs could be obtained *only* through a doctor's prescription, while milder drugs considered safer—and perceived by many consumers as consequently less effective—could still be purchased "over the counter" without a prescription.

This gave doctors considerable power regarding the choice, purchase and use of various drugs by their patients. To sell their products, pharmaceutical companies needed to sell their drugs not to the end user nearly so much as to the "middleman", the doctor who would prescribe them.

The DSM-I

Also in 1952, the American Psychiatric Association published their first *Diagnostic and Statistical Manual: Mental Disorders* (DSM-I), a "clinically-useful" guide to identifying and classifying different types of mental illness, intended for psychiatrists, psychologists, and general practitioners. It was based on two earlier guides, one developed by the US Army in 1945, and the other by the World Health Organisation (WHO) in 1949. Both of those were probably influenced by Kraepelin's work earlier in the century. The DSM-I divided psychiatric illness into three main categories: psychosis (hallucinations and delusions—out of touch with reality), neurosis (depression, anxiety, envy, guilt—in touch with reality, but not liking it), and behavioural reactions or personality disorders (e.g., sexual deviation, alcoholism, compulsive personality disorders).

The DSM-I assumed these various conditions resulted as a *reaction* to life's circumstances. Significantly, the word "reaction" was removed from subsequent editions of the DSM as the theory of bio-medical causation for mental illness evolved.

The first neuroleptics (anti-psychotics)

1952 was a big year for SKF too, the year in which they secured the US patent rights for a new drug, chlorpromazine. Synthesized a year earlier by the French pharmaceutical company Rhône-Poulenc, the drug enabled surgery patients to remain conscious while rendered indifferent to procedures being performed upon them. Touted as "a new vegetative stabilizer" by Henri Laborit in his 1952 paper, the drug also showed promise as a way of controlling psychiatric patients' aggressive and disruptive behaviours without causing sleepiness.[20]

SKF marketed chlorpromazine under the trade name Thorazine (it was called Largactil in France where, incidentally, it sold for about 1/6th what SKF charged for it in the US[21]), and compared it favourably with the frontal lobotomy, highlighting the drug's ability to render psychotic patients "immobile" and "emotionally indifferent".[22] Never mind that the most common patient experience of taking Thorazine was to feel "like a zombie" or "confused" or "alienated from myself,"[23] or that the drug caused a distressing feeling of inner anxiety, movement disorders and drooling. Thorazine was, after all, not being sold to patients but to those who had to "manage" those patients. With a new patented drug now available to treat it, the diagnosis of schizophrenia became increasingly common.

In 1954, the US FDA approved the widespread use of Thorazine. To promote use of the drug, SKF produced a TV show *The March of Medicine* in which they outlined how carefully Thorazine had been tested, and *Time* magazine produced a complimentary article on Thorazine aimed at the general public. Meanwhile, SKF and other drug companies began lobbying in Washington for increased government funding for research into drug treatments for the mentally ill.[24]

Psychiatric pharmaceuticals, they argued, could shorten psychiatric hospital stays, and perhaps render them completely unnecessary for all but the most extreme cases, thus saving taxpayers' money. With the right drugs, family and community care could virtually replace expensive hospital care for the mentally ill. It must have been an effective appeal because Federal spending on mental health research in the US increased ten-fold in the seven years between 1953 and 1961.[25]

Another so-called antipsychotic drug—actually, the term neuroleptic was more commonly used in the mid-1900s, from the Greek words *neuron* (nerve) and *lambanō* (take hold of)—that received less attention was reserpine. Isolated from the dried roots of Indian snakeroot (*rauvolfia serpentina*), this was a folk-medicine that had been used for centuries in India for a variety of health problems ranging from insanity to snakebite. Reserpine became available in the US in the mid-1950s, where it was used to control high blood pressure as well as for psychosis.

In the first ever modern-style drug trial, Michael Shepherd compared reserpine to placebo (a non-active treatment) with a group of depressed patients in 1955 and found the drug demonstrated an anti-depressive action superior to any other drug available at the time. In spite of this, pharmaceutical company Ciba decided to market the drug as an antipsychotic instead, to compete directly with SKF's popular Thorazine, for a share of the neuroleptic market.[26]

The stimulants

Meanwhile, with the patent for Benzedrine Sulphate running out (meaning they could no longer have exclusive rights to marketing or the ability to set the price of the drug), SKF introduced a new amphetamine-derivative drug (with a new patent) in the 1950s called Dexamyl, composed of dextroamphetamine and the barbiturate amobarbital. It was promoted as a product to quell anxiety and alleviate depression without drowsiness, and also as a remedy for weight loss which would not only lessen the appetite but also treat the emotional causes of overeating. The drug was promoted to doctors as ideal to "help the depressed and anxiety-ridden housewife surrounded by a monotonous routine of daily problems."[27]

While not technically an amphetamine, Ritalin (methylphenidate) was another stimulant that also came onto the market in the 1950s. Synthesized in 1944 by Swiss pharmaceutical company Ciba, it was initially used for chronic fatigue and narcolepsy, a sleep disorder. The US FDA approved it for use in 1955, but it would not become a household name until the 1980s. More on that later.

The first tranquilizers

Meprobamate was developed by Frank Berger in the 1950s as a muscle relaxant for laboratory animals, and its potential for sales in the human anxiety market quickly became apparent. Promising a sense of relaxation without the sedation engendered by the barbiturates, meprobamate was seen as a perfect choice for the neurotic patient at home. Berger coined a new term for the product: *tranquilizer*. It was marketed under the trade names *Miltown* and *Equanil* by Carter Products and it became the first blockbuster psychotropic drug in history[28].

As with SKF's Dexamyl, much of the advertising promoted the drug as providing relief for women struggling with the rigours of ordinary life: "relieves premenstrual tension," "pregnancy can be a happier experience," and "for the tense and nervous patient, relief comes fast and comfortably" (the advertising illustration shows a harried-looking woman overlaid by a peaceful one)[29]. By 1957, a third of all the drug prescription sales in America were for Miltown and Equanil[30] and *Consumer Reports* reported that one American in twenty was taking tranquilizers[31].

The MAOI antidepressants

Meanwhile, back in 1951, two new compounds, iproniazid and isoniazid, were synthesized by the pharmaceutical company Hoffman-La Roche from leftover World War II stockpiles of hydrazine, a key component used in German rocket fuel. These compounds were tested on tubercular patients, and the results caused considerable excitement. By Easter 1952 (this was before the legal requirement of clinical trials), headlines proclaimed iproniazid (in particular) a "TB wonder drug."[32]

One unexpected side effect of iproniazid treatment for tuberculosis was the sense of euphoria or hypomania experienced by some patients. Recognizing the potential of the new drug as a possible treatment for depression, psychiatrist Nathan Kline and his colleagues trialled it with 20 long-term institutionalized "probably schizophrenic" patients and found it effective[33].

Iproniazid was the first monoamine oxidase inhibitor (MAOI) antidepressant (although the term *antidepressant* didn't exist then—that word first appeared in 1959 in the *New York Times,* about the same time as the next antidepressant type—the tricyclics—hit the market[34]). In spite of their propensity to cause liver damage and what became known as the "cheese reaction" whereby co-consumption with fermented food such as cheese or wine could result in a sudden and potentially-fatal episode of hypertension, MAOIs were prescribed for depression during the 1950s and early 1960s, especially within the hospital environment where food consumption could be easily monitored. Their use declined with the advent of safer drugs and more frequent outpatient care for depression, and they are rarely used today.[35]

Armed with a model of mental illness as a physical disease, a medical protocol of disease diagnosis followed by treatment, and a small but poised-to-grow pharmacopeia of drugs for the treatment of psychosis/schizophrenia (Thorazine), depression (Dexamyl and the MAOIs) and anxiety (Miltown, Equanil, and Dexamyl), the pill-popping 1950s saw the second half of the 20th century headed firmly down the path of chemical fixes for almost everyone, and a meteoric rise in financial fortunes for pharmaceutical companies. By 1958, SKF was identified by *Fortune* magazine as having the 2nd highest net profit (over 33% return) of all American industrial corporations[36].

The modern tranquilizers

The development of the benzodiazepines, the *modern* tranquilizers, began with Leo Sternbach, a molecular chemist working for the chemical research company Hoffmann-La Roche. One of the compounds he synthesized, chlordiazepoxide, was found to have clinically significant hypnotic and sedative effects. In spite of dubious safety results with initial (albeit limited) trials, it was brought to the market in 1960, and that release was followed by the still-popular diazepam (Valium) in 1963 and lorazepam in 1972[37]. A number of other "benzos" were also brought to the market as patents for barbiturate products lapsed, launching what came to be known as the 20th century "Age of Anxiety".

Heavily promoted with direct-to-consumer advertising in popular women's magazines such as *The Ladies Home Journal* and *Cosmopolitan* and featured in articles in respectable news magazines such as *Time, Newsweek* and *Science Digest* as a panacea for the suburban frustrations of modern housewifery, the benzos became known as "Mother's Little Helper" epitomized by the 1965 Rolling Stones song by the same name:

*"Kids are different today, I hear ev'ry mother say
Mother needs something today to calm her down
And though she's not really ill, there's a little
yellow pill
She goes running for the shelter of a mother's
little helper
And it helps her on her way, gets her through her
busy day..."*

Freudian psychoanalysis, still tremendously popular in the 1960s, might help identify problems, but Valium promised to fix them. Reports of "improved sleep," frigid women...responding more readily to their husbands' advances" and "calm in frantic lives" saw sales soar, signifying the strength of the new idea of chemical interventions over the more involved and costly process of psychoanalysis in psychiatry[38] or, indeed, for simply dealing with the everyday ups and downs of ordinary life.

Tricyclic antidepressants

The development of imipramine, the first tricyclic antidepressant drug (so-called because of its three-ring chemical structure), also began in the early 1950s when the Swiss chemical company Geigy was searching for a product to rival Rhône-Poulenc's and SKF's new anti-psychotic chlorpromazine. They went digging into their archives of chemical compounds and examined one developed in the 1800s for the German textile dye industry. Identified as similar in chemical structure to chlorpromazine, Geigy set out to see what it would do when tested on psychiatric patients.

Swiss psychiatrist Roland Kuhn trialled the drug with patients and found imapramine unsuitable as an anti-psychotic—it worsened the patients' conditions—but the compound did show some promise when he tried it with depressed patients. It was brought to the market in the late 1950s in Europe first, and shortly thereafter in North America, but was not actively promoted. Geigy, like Ciba with reserpine, did not recognize the market potential for an antidepressant and continued searching for a rival for the profit-star chlorpromazine[39].

The drug company Merck wasn't so short-sighted. They approached Frank Ayd, Nathan Kline (the developer of the MAOI iproniazid) and several of their colleagues and asked them to examine amitriptyline. Like imapramine, amitriptyline was based on a tricyclic structure, and Merck wanted to know if it would be useful with patients suffering from schizophrenia or depression. When the depression trials proved positive, Merck filed a patent in 1961 for the drug as a depression treatment, and then set about marketing depression to create a market for the product[40].

Frank Ayd wrote a book titled *Recognizing the Depressed Patient*, and in a clever move, Merck commissioned fifty thousand copies for distribution to psychiatrists and physicians in the areas where the new drug was being actively promoted. Amitriptyline quickly became the best-selling antidepressant as there was no dangerous "cheese reaction" as with the MAOIs. Amitriptyline remains the best-selling tricyclic antidepressant available today.

Legalities and drug testing

Until the early 1960s, pharmaceutical companies had been relatively free to investigate new chemical compounds by first testing them on animals and then having a doctor or psychiatrist try out the new drugs on sick patients to find out what they did. If there was any indication of drug effectiveness—or even if there wasn't—the compounds could be patented and launched on to the market.

This changed after the thalidomide disaster in the early 1960s, when pregnant mothers were given a new hypnotic (sleeping tablet) and anti-nausea drug that resulted in more than 10,000 babies being born with severe birth defects. Thalidomide was pulled off the market in 1962. Responding to the public outcry, government regulators around the world put into place new regulations requiring drug testing for safety prior to marketing.

In 1962, the US FDA amended the 1938 Food, Drug and Cosmetic Act to require not only that new drugs be tested for safety, but that clinical trials be used to prove that drug was actually effective for treating a particular condition. Although this extended the time involved in bringing a new drug to market, and raised the bar a bit regarding efficacy, the FDA only required two trials demonstrating a drug's superiority to placebo (no treatment), and data from any unsuccessful trials—regardless of how many there might be—was not required to be lodged.

Figuring out how the drugs work

Up until this point, drug discovery had been a relatively hit-and-miss affair. To discover how to make more marketable drugs for depression, anxiety and psychosis, researchers needed to understand *why* the existing drugs seemed to work. What was it the pills were doing, exactly? The identification of neurotransmitters, the chemicals that transmit information between brain synapses, prompted the amine theories.

In the 1960s, American Joseph Schildkraut proposed the theory that depression is caused by a deficit of catecholamines. Catecholamines are organic chemical compounds produced by the body that function both as neurotransmitters (chemical messengers operating between neurons), and as hormones (released by endocrine glands into the bloodstream for widespread delivery and effect).

The most common catecholamines in humans are epinephrine (adrenalin), norepinephrine (noradrenalin) and dopamine. Schildkraut believed that low levels of norepinephrine, in particular, caused depression, and he based his theory on the belief that drugs such as reserpine deplete or deactivate production of norepinephrine and produce sedation and depression, whereas drugs such as imapramine and the MAOIs increase brain levels of norepinephrine and in doing so seem to stimulate activity and uplift mood[41]. Bizarrely, he apparently ignored the 1955 clinical trial that showed reserpine's effectiveness *against* depression.

Around the same time, in the UK, George Ashcroft found lowered levels of the monoamine serotonin, also a hormone and neurotransmitter, in the spinal fluid of depressed patients and in the cadavers of suicides. He hypothesized that depression might be caused by low levels of serotonin, although he later rescinded that theory following further research.[42]

True or not, either hypothesis was a boon to the pharmaceutical industry because it suggested that depression could be sold as a medical illness with a clear chemical/biological cause, and medication to "fix" the biological "fault" could be developed. If depression was caused by low levels of key amines such as norepinephrine or serotonin, and new antidepressants could be shown to boost those low levels, the prospects for marketing and sales would be enormous.

More than fifty years on, the chemical imbalance theory of depression, and the suggestion that depression results from a deficiency of key amine neurotransmitters—either serotonin or norepinephrine—remains widely reported but unsupported by any scientific evidence.[43]

The same sort of theory was also developed to explain the "success" of the anti-psychotic drugs chlorpromazine and reserpine. In 1963, Swedish pharmacologist Arvid Carlsson discovered that these drugs inhibit the catecholamine dopamine by shutting down dopaminergic pathways in the brain. From that observation, he deduced that if that is what the drugs do, and if they help control patients' psychotic symptoms, then the cause of schizophrenia must be too much dopamine in the brain.

Since dopamine is essential for normal motor movement, it is not surprising that anti-psychotic medications also produced Parkinsonian side effects when given to schizophrenic patients. These side effects include tremor, stiffness, rigidity of muscles, and a slowing of movement—symptoms of Parkinson's Disease, which is caused by—surprise, surprise—low levels of dopamine. The drugs also disabled the brain's limbic system which regulates emotions, resulting in psychotic patients becoming more apathetic when taking anti-psychotic drugs. Although often distressing for patients, these side effects of the drugs often make patients more manageable for caregivers.

Problems with the anti-psychotics

Moving psychotic patients back into the community, according to many advocates, hinged upon keeping them medicated. Few patients found Thorazine pleasant to take, and one 1965 study suggested that nearly half of patients discontinued their prescribed medication once released from hospital[44]. The solution to this problem was a long-acting injectable drug.

Two new products, haloperidol, first synthesized in 1958 by Janssen Laboratories in Belgium, and Prolixin (fluphenazine), brought to the market in the 1960s by Bristol-Myers Squibb, were more powerful than chlorpromazine and could be given by injection. Regular injections every two to three weeks ensured forgetful or reluctant patients would remain compliant with doctor-prescribed long-term maintenance treatment whether they wanted to take the drugs or not.

Over the next few years, many pharmaceutical companies developed their own patented antipsychotic drugs to be administered orally or by injection. These included loxapine, molindone, perphenazine, flupentixol and half a dozen others. Some of these drugs have subsequently been removed from the market, or are only available in some countries.

Parkinsonian side effects were not the only reason many patients disliked taking the anti-psychotics. Neuroleptic-Induced Deficit Syndrome (NIDS) refers to the variety of drug-induced disorders caused by the use of neuroleptic drugs. Besides Parkinsonian symptoms, which may affect as many as two-thirds of patients with long-term or high-dose use, and symptoms strongly resembling encephalitis lethargica (lethargy, apathy, catatonia) (see the film *Awakenings* for a Hollywood-ized portrayal of this disease), the drugs also cause many users to experience tardive dyskinesia (repetitive involuntary muscle movements or twitches), akathisia (inner restlessness and anxiety), blunted emotions, memory loss, weight gain, sexual dysfunction, seizures, rashes, and blood disorders[45]. Nevertheless, chlorpromazine (Thorazine), haloperidol, and fluphenazine became mainstays of drug treatment for schizophrenic patients for the next several decades, and remain in common use today.

SSRI antidepressants

The tricyclic antidepressants—most pharmaceutical companies patented their own versions—dominated the antidepressant market until the mid-1980s when the first Selective Serotonin Reuptake Inhibitors (SSRIs) were launched. Whereas the tricyclics and the MAOIs were discovered more-or-less by accident, the SSRIs were a deliberate creation.

While Schildkraut's 1965 catecholamine theory pointed to the accretion of norepinephrine as the essential *modus operandi* of antidepressant drug function, Swedish researcher Arvid Carlsson proposed that antidepressant compounds that would act selectively on the serotonin system might be as effective as the tricyclics and have fewer side effects[46].

In 1978 he trialled two new chemical compounds designed to disrupt the natural flow of serotonin between nerve cells by inhibiting the discharging cell's natural ability to "uptake" unused serotonin and thereby leaving an excess in the synapse, the gap between the two cells. Zimelidine and citalopram were tested first on rats and then in human trials.

Zimelidine was launched onto the European market as Zelmid in 1982, becoming the world's first commercially-available SSRI, but was removed shortly thereafter following reports linking it to development of the paralyzing neurological disease Guillain Barré syndrome, liver damage, and suicidal ideation[47]. Citalopram was not made commercially available until 1989 in Europe and 1998 in the US, and only after the phenomenal success of the first blockbuster SSRI, Prozac.

Prozac (fluoxetine) was launched onto the US market in 1987. In his book *Let Them Eat Prozac*, David Healy tells the story of the development of this drug, and I'll summarized that story here because I think it is an interesting and revealing tale.

In the 1970s, Eli Lilly Pharmaceuticals needed to develop a new antidepressant drug to replace their best-selling tricyclic antidepressant nortriptyline, marketed under the trade name Pamalor, soon to lose patent protection. They played around with existing drugs a bit and adapted a variant of the antihistamine diphenhydramine (trade name Benadryl) to create a new chemical compound that looked interesting. Although it did not block the sedative action of reserpine as tricyclic and MAOI antidepressants did, they found it did stimulate aggression in rats and dogs. That suggested to Lilly that it had "activating" properties.

Unfortunately, the new drug did not show efficacy for use with severe depression, causing distress and agitation in patients. Nor did it work when they tested it for schizophrenia, pain relief, hypertension, or obesity. Finally, adjuncted with benzodiazepines (tranquilizers) to quell subjects' ensuing agitation, it was trialled with a group of five mildly depressed individuals.[48] All five responded positively (although how much of that positive response might have been due to the benzodiazepine we will never know). It was a small success, but enough to initiate the launch of what some consider the biggest blockbuster drug of all time.

Fluoxetine underwent numerous clinical trials over the next few years. The FDA requires lodgement of two trials demonstrating superiority of the drug over placebo (no medication), while data from unsuccessful trials need not be lodged[49]. Of the three placebo-controlled trials Lilly submitted to the FDA for fluoxetine, one showed no effect, one showed a small superiority over placebo but inferiority to the tricyclic imipramine, and the third showed efficacy but only had eleven completers of the four-week trial[50]. Furthermore, Lilly trial subjects who experienced drug-induced agitation were given benzodiazapines during the trials, although this was not reported in the published results.[51]

We know in retrospect the trials also highlighted issues over drug-induced suicidality and other disturbing symptoms, but researchers overcame that obstacle to approval by coding such issues in the results under the general banner "symptoms of depression" rather than as a separate category.[52] Lilly's results were adequate (but just barely) for the drug to receive FDA approval in 1987.

The Eli Lilly marketing team launched the drug—now branded as Prozac, a "catchy" name with connotations of favourable (pro) and energy/zippy/relaxed (zac)—onto the American market in 1987 with much fanfare, touting its one-pill-a-day-fits-everybody profile in an attempt to expand beyond the psychiatric prescribing market into the much larger sales arena of general practitioners. Promoted as "a breakthrough drug in the treatment of depression," Prozac made the cover of *Newsweek* in 1990.[53]

Ironically, it took six more years for the drug to pass German regulators for use there, one regulator noting, "Considering the benefit and risk, we think this preparation totally unsuitable for depression."[54] Nevertheless, Prozac proved enormously popular, with sales for that one drug alone accounting for 30% of Eli Lilly's company profits.[55] Although the patent for the drug expired in 2001, generic fluoxetine remains a popular antidepressant choice for many doctors and patients today.

Several other SSRIs soon joined fluoxetine on the US and European markets, each company wanting its own patented SSRI drug to grab their share of this lucrative market: GlaxoSmithKline (SKF had now mutated into GSK) had Paxil (paroxetine), Pfizer had Zoloft (sertraline), Forest Laboratories had Celexa (citalopram), and so on. Touted as safer than tricyclics because of lower cardio-toxic reactions in overdose, and safer than MAOIs with their liver toxicity and "cheese reaction", very easy for general practitioners to prescribe, and applicable to an ever-growing list of applications both on- and off-label (depression, anxiety, pain relief, eating disorders) SSRIs have gone on to dominate the antidepressant drug market for decades.

The DSM-III and DSM-IV

With so many drugs on the market, and psychiatric prescribing increasingly falling into the hands of general practitioners, a standardized guide to diagnosis was essential. The first *Diagnostic and Statistical Manual of Mental Disorders* (DSM-I) had been published in 1952, and a revised but similar DSM-II in 1968. When the DSM-III was published in 1980 (with a further revision in 1987), it had been transformed from a fairly simple guide (the DSM-II was 92 pages long) to a substantial and convoluted 482 page tome with 265 possible diagnoses on offer for the puzzled psychiatric or GP diagnostician. In spite of its unwieldy nature, the manual proved so popular that book sales led to the formation of the American Psychiatric Press.[56]   The DSM-III was almost certainly pivotal in helping to shift psychiatry from a biopsychosocial framework to a medical model.[57]

By the time the DSM-IV was published in 1994, the number of psychiatric disorders had grown to nearly 300, and the manual had expanded to 886 pages. The book divided psychiatric diagnosis into five dimensions, or axes, that included not only diagnoses for conditions such as depression, anxiety, schizophrenia, autism spectrum disorders, and eating disorders (I mention only a few here) but also for mental retardation; disorders resulting from physical injury, psychosocial and environmental factors; and disorders affecting children. The DSM does not offer advice for treatment.

The somewhat controversial[58] DSM-V, published in 2013, is roughly the same size as the DSM-IV.

Medication for kids

One prescribing area that was ripe for exploitation by the pharmaceutical companies was the paediatric population. Until 1980, giving psychiatric medication to children outside of an institutional environment was rare. That began to change with the publication of the new DSM-III which included, among its many new diagnoses, Attention Deficit Disorder (ADD), with or without hyperactivity; in the 1987 revision this became two distinct diagnoses, ADD (i.e., without hyperactivity) and ADHD (Attention Deficit Hyperactivity Disorder).

Of course, children who were aggressive, inattentive, prone to mischief, and defiant of authority were not a new phenomenon. Some children are just excessively lively by nature, and certain environments and experiences can exacerbate negative behaviours. Furthermore, following the viral encephalitis lethargica epidemic in the 1920s, many of the children who recovered afterwards exhibited disturbing and aggressive behaviours which were attributed by doctors to disease-caused brain damage. These sorts of behaviours in their extreme manifestations had previously been categorized as "minimal brain dysfunction" or "organic brain syndrome".[59] With the advent of ADD and ADHD labels, however, psychiatrists, doctors, teachers and parents had a way to describe modern children without discernible brain damage who nevertheless presented difficult-to-manage behavioural problems in the home and school environments. Could the pharmaceutical industry come up with a pill for that?

There was a precedent for treating childhood hyperactivity with stimulant drugs. In 1937, psychiatrist Charles Bradley trialled SKF's Benzedrine Sulphate for a few weeks on a group of institutionalized children, aged 5 to 14, with behavioural disorders. He found about half of the irritable, aggressive, noisy children became (surprisingly, paradoxically) more subdued, placid and helpful when given the drug, while the other children were "stimulated" as anticipated and showed increased alertness and initiative.[60] The medical community didn't pay much attention to Bradley's findings at the time, but after the publication of the new DSM-III, his observations seemed useful.

The new diagnosis for inattentive, impulsive, fidgety children was great news for pharmaceutical company Ciba-Geigy who recognized a huge new market for their drug Ritalin (methylpenidate). To market both the condition and the drug, they helped fund a parent support group for hyperactive kids (CHADD—Children and Adults with Attention Deficit Disorder) that went on to lobby the US congress to get the condition declared a "disability" and therefore eligible for government-funded special services in the US; they were successful in 1991.[61] Between 1991 and 1999, Ritalin sales increased by 500%,[62] and by 2000 an estimated 7 million children had been prescribed the drug.[63] Children who did not respond so well to Ritalin were often given amphetamines instead.

With the philosophical barrier of medicating kids-at-home with psychiatric drugs breached, pharmaceutical companies looked to expand existing products into the new and lucrative paediatric market. Ritalin operates as a dopamine reuptake inhibiter; SSRIs operate as serotonin reuptake inhibitors. Children and teenagers, pharmaceutical marketers reasoned, can suffer from depression just as easily as adults can. Whereas in 1988, one in 250 American children under the age of 19 was prescribed a drug for depression, with the advent of the SSRIs (remember: one pill fits all) and the precedent of ADD and ADHD medication for kids, by 2002 one out of every 40 children in the US was taking an antidepressant[64].

Eli Lilly was the only pharmaceutical company able to get their SSRI (Prozac) officially approved by the US FDA for use within the paediatric population[65], but any of the SSRIs and other antidepressants could be proscribed to children and teenagers off-label (see more on off-label prescribing in the next section). The National Institute for Health and Care Excellence (NICE) in the UK does not recommend the use of

SSRIs for children, but have not been so hesitant in setting guidelines for the prescription of antipsychotics for young patients[66].

The uptake of antipsychotic drugs for the paediatric group showed a similar profile to antidepressants. The Texas Medication Algorithm Project (TMAP) was begun in the US in the 1990s. Funded by pharmaceutical companies, it sought to create treatment consensus on the prescribing of antipsychotics, initially for schizophrenia and later for bipolar disorder. Several American states ruled that TMAP (or similar) guidelines be applied on patients receiving care in public facilities or through government insurance companies.

In 1999, the state of Texas endorsed the TMAP treatment guidelines for children as well as adults, even though no antipsychotic drug treatments had been approved by the FDA for use with minors. By 2004, Texas Medicaid spending on antipsychotics had increased more than six-fold, with tens of thousands of children and adolescents prescribed antipsychotic medications. By 2009, children treated under a government Medicaid program anywhere in the US were four times more likely to receive antipsychotics than children not covered by Medicaid.[67] In the UK, NICE follows a similar protocol to TMAP.[68]

Off label prescribing

Medications are often prescribed "off label", meaning they are prescribed for indications for which they have not been approved or licensed, prescribed to patients who have not been approved to receive them, or prescribed at dosage levels beyond approved levels. Pharmaceutical companies actively promote off-label prescribing, although doing so is illegal, tossing off court fines as part of the cost of doing business. Pfizer, for example, paid US$2.75 billion in fines for off-label drug promotion between 2004 and 2009, just over 1% of the company's impressive $245 billion revenue.[69]

More recently, in 2012 GSK paid out $3 billion to settle claims over their antidepressant paroxetine (Paxil) for unlawful promotion, kickbacks, and concealing negative data from drug trial reports, and in 2013 Johnson & Johnson paid out nearly $2.2 billion to settle claims over their anti-psychotic Risperdal (illegal marketing and payment of kickbacks to doctors).[70]

In many countries, including the US, it is not illegal for a doctor to prescribe medication off-label, nor is it compulsory that the patient be informed that a prescribed drug is not approved for a particular use, but the issue creates ethical and liability conundrums. In other countries, while off-label prescribing isn't illegal, doctors are required to inform patients of potential risks and benefits of taking a medication outside of approved guidelines. Because of cross-over advertising, however, many doctors are unaware of which indications are tested and approved for a drug and which are not.

The most common type of off-label prescribing occurs with paediatric patients, elderly patients, patients who become pregnant, and patients with contraindicated disorders or medications. All of the SSRI antidepressants, for example, have been prescribed off-label to children and the elderly, and to adults for a variety of off-label conditions including pain relief, insomnia, premature ejaculation, migraine headaches, fibromyalgia, irritable bowel syndrome, chronic fatigue, and ADD[71].

Bipolar

Another new diagnosis that showed up in the DSM-III was "bipolar", although it had been noted for centuries that occasionally individuals experienced not only depressive lows but also euphoric highs in cycles. Kraepelin categorized this as part of the general mania-to-depression continuum in the 1800s, and identified it as a rare mood fluctuation disorder that generally self-resolved itself with time.

German psychiatrist Karl Leonhard first used the term "bipolar" in 1957 when he tagged it as a separate condition from unipolar depression or mania. At that time, it was estimated to affect perhaps one in every 13,000 people,[72] and until the DSM-III was published, the condition got little attention. Today, bipolar disorder officially affects one person in forty in the U.S, a conundrum that author Robert Whitaker explores in his excellent book *Anatomy of an Epidemic*[73] and David Healy addresses in his excellent *Mania: A Short History of Bipolar Disorder*.[74]

Several factors partly explain that increase. The DSM-III raised awareness of the condition of course, but it also stipulated that the depressive or manic episodes must be severe enough to require hospitalization. Today, hospitalization is not a prerequisite for the diagnosis, and just two days of mania coupled with a depressive episode is adequate for a diagnosis of bipolar.[75]

There is evidence that prior psychoactive drug use—illicit or prescription—significantly increases the risk of developing a bipolar mood disorder, and antidepressant use is particularly implicated.[76] Since many patients diagnosed as bipolar were initially diagnosed as depressed and given antidepressant medication, it is not surprising that many depressed patients are later relabelled as bipolar.

Regardless of the diagnostic label plastered onto a patient, however, pharmaceutical companies are quick to recognize a market and provide treatment options. In recent years, bipolar diagnoses for juvenile patients—prior to 1991 it was barely considered possible for children to be considered bipolar prior to puberty—have broadened the commercial market for medications and increased the population percentage of bipolar sufferers.

Lithium was the treatment of choice for bipolar patients in the 1980s—remember Australian John Cade's study in 1949?—but being a natural product, no pharmaceutical company could patent it so it was not widely promoted and few tests or trials were done. Indeed, the US FDA had banned the drug because of cardiac toxicity in 1949,[77] but twenty-one years later decided to approve it for use with manic depression.

Initially lithium was reported to produce a fairly good response in controlling patients' bipolar symptoms, although many complained of minds feeling dulled and movements slowed. Discontinuation usually resulted in relapse (or withdrawal symptoms which mimic relapse), but the prognosis for long-term outcomes with prolonged used was equally discouraging, the drug affecting other body organs besides the brain.

If lithium was found unsuitable for a patient, anticonvulsants such as valproate (Depakote) could be tried, although these too have side effects, as could anti-psychotic drugs. Several of the newer atypical antipsychotic drugs (see the upcoming section on second generation drugs) have been approved for use with bipolar patients. Rebranded as "mood stabilizers" rather than "anti-psychotics" to moderate the negative connotation associated with psychosis, these are the most common drug treatments used today for bipolar patients.

Patent expiration

Drug patents in the US are generally good for 17-20 years. A patent allows the pharmaceutical company to "own" the drug preparation and set their own drug charges, which is assumed to be an appropriate reward for the time, cost, and effort required to develop new drugs. Once a drug company loses patent protection, however, the drug can be sold as a "generic" drug by any company that wants to manufacture it for whatever price they want to charge. Prozac, for example, fell from about US$2.50 per pill, when it came off Eli Lilly's patent protection in 2001, to about 20¢ per pill as generic fluoxetine, which was enough to cover ingredient and production costs and still generate a profit for the manufacturer—an interesting indicator of the profit margins possible for patented pharmaceuticals.

To enable high-priced drug sales for as long as possible, pharmaceutical companies have a vested interest in getting drugs on the market as quickly as they can. Often they create "new" patented products that are really "re-jigs" of old products—which is cheaper and faster than developing completely new drugs. Examples include controlled-release (CR) versions of existing drugs like GSK's Paxil (paroxetine), minor tweaking of the chemical structure of an existing drug to make a new one (e.g. venlafaxine and desvenlafaxine), and the re-vamping of old drugs for new indications, such as Eli Lilly's new patent for Prozac, reincarnated as a purple pill and marketed it as Serafem, a "new drug treatment" for Premenstrual Dysphoric Disorder[78] (what most of us call PMS: that grumpy patch many women experience a few days before they get their period). Many women prescribed Serafem had no idea they were actually being prescribed Prozac, an antidepressant[79].

Another route to financial prosperity can be created through branding. Prozac as a name was so effective, it became a household word almost synonymous with antidepressant, just as Beyer's "aspirin" (acetylsalicylic acid just doesn't have the same ring) or "Kleenex" tissues have rocketed brand names into common use as generic terms.

We all know that people will pay more for designer jeans or shoes than they will for no-brand or nobody's-every-heard-of-it brands even if the no-brand item is of similar quality and considerably cheaper than the item with the recognized and "valued" name. The same is true for medications. Lilly's Prozac carries more prestige and perceived "authenticity" than generic fluoxetine, and patients will often opt for the branded over the unbranded product even at more than ten times the price of the generic version.

Second generation drugs

With patents expiring for antipsychotic drugs and SSRIs, drug manufacturers also needed to create new products, new patents, and new patients to keep company profits rolling in.

The atypical antipsychotics, sometimes referred to as second-generation antipsychotics, were first introduced in the 1990s. Because the new drugs affected a variety of neuron receptors with less emphasis on the dopamine receptor than earlier antipsychotic drugs, the negative effect on motor movement caused by "typical" antipsychotics were mitigated, although tardive dyskinesia remained a problem and risk of weight gain and diabetes was increased with their use compared to the older "typical" antipsychotics.

The drugs were otherwise deemed similar in effectiveness to the older drugs when used to treat schizophrenia, and many are also approved for treatment of mania and bipolar. Atypical antipsychotics include clozapine (Clozaril), olanzapine (Zyprexa), quetiapine (Seroquel), risperidone (Risperdal), and ziprasidone (Geodon).

Atypical antidepressants were also brought to the market In the 1990s. These included the SNRIs (Serotonin Norepinephrine Reuptake Inhibitors) such as duloxetine (Cymbalta) and venlafaxine (Effexor); venlafaxine also inhibits the reuptake of dopamine. Another atypical, Mirtazapine (Remeron), is a tetracyclic (as opposed to a tricyclic) and affects the uptake of serotonin, norepinephrine and histamine between cells.

GSK's Bupropion (Wellbutrin) inhibits dopamine and norepinephrine reuptake but does not affect serotonin; it is also marketed as a smoking-cessation aid under the brand name Zyban. And there are others—it's not a particularly homogenous group of drugs.

The modern antidepressants—tricyclics, SSRIs and atypicals—affect a variety of neurotransmitters in a variety of ways, but there are no stand-out performers. All of the antidepressants have issues with side effects and withdrawal, and none have demonstrated anything beyond marginal efficacy compared to placebo in trials.

Drug side effects and withdrawal

Taking psychiatric drugs causes changes in the user's brain and body which can result in a variety of side effects that may be concerning to patients or their families. If you are taking a psychiatric drug, or thinking about taking a psychiatric drug, a quick perusal on the internet—search under the drug name (and generic name if that's different) and "side effects"—will reveal what is officially confirmed as a side effect for the drug.

Remember that many people who experience minor side effects from a drug often don't report on their experience, and even significant reports don't become "official" unless your doctor passes on your concerns to reporting bodies, so the official information almost certainly underestimates side effect frequency.

In some cases, side effects may not be immediately evident or visible. As an example, analysis of longitudinal studies (that is, studies that occur over an extended period of time) suggest that antipsychotic drugs used for an extended period cause a loss of brain tissue[80].

In the event you are taking several drugs, it can often be hard to sift out which drug might be causing what problems, or whether any of the problems is caused by two or more drugs interacting in a negative way. Also because each of us is different, we each have different reactions to certain drugs. Where one drug might cause headaches or nausea for some users, that same drug might cause an increase in irritability, euphoria, sexual dysfunction or suicidal thoughts in others. For some, side effects might be minor annoyances, while for others they may be debilitating. Some people experience no discernible side effects at all.

It is useful to remember that just because a drug is marketed as a psychiatric drug does not mean only the brain is affected by it. As an example, the SSRI antidepressants affect the reuptake of serotonin between cells. While the pharmaceutical industry is quick to tell you that this can enhance your mood by altering how your brain processes serotonin, they rarely go on to tell you that only about 10% of the body's serotonin is in the brain. The majority (over 80%) is found in the digestive tract where it affects the amount and quality of mucus and facilitates digestion and the movement of waste products through the intestines[81]. Serotonin also affects the body's immune system, blood circulation, blood pressure, and blood platelet aggregation[82], and plays an active role in sexual function[83]. When you take an SSRI, you disrupt normal cell functioning throughout your entire body, not just in your brain.

Anti-psychotics increase the risk of heart attacks, stroke, diabetes and suicide for patients who take them, while significantly shortening life expectancy rates[84].

Many people, perhaps most, experience problems when discontinuing a psychiatric drug, especially if they have been taking it for a long time. Although these can be relatively minor withdrawal symptoms that pass within a week or two, sometimes the withdrawal experience can be more disturbing, distressing, prolonged, and sometimes even dangerous.

If someone has been taking a drug for a while, their body and brain have adapted and altered in the presence of those chemicals because they change how the brain and body function[85]. When the drug is no longer being delivered into the body, the whole system needs time to readjust and resume the natural processes that allowed it to function normally.

If you are thinking about coming off any form of psychiatric medication yourself, it is important to consult with your doctor first. You will probably want to decrease the dose very slowly over weeks or months to give your brain and body time to adjust to lesser quantities of the medication. Let family and friends know when you are adjusting the dose so they can offer you support and encouragement should you need it. This is also a good safety measure as occasionally withdrawal can cause emotional instability or volatile mood changes that may cause you to think and behave in unexpected ways. If a drop in dose does cause a strong reaction, you can always resume the previous dose and after you have stabilized for a few days, you can titrate down with smaller decreases.

These brief comments on psychiatric drug withdrawal only give a very broad-brush picture of the process. Two useful books that further expand on this subject are Dr. Peter Breggin's *Psychiatric Drug Withdrawal: A Guide for Researchers, Therapists, Patients and Their Families* and Dr. Joseph Glenmullen's *The Antidepressant Solution: A Step-by-Step Guide to Safely Overcoming Antidepressant Withdrawal, Dependence, and "Addiction"*. The former is written more for health professionals than for patients and covers a broader spectrum of drugs, while the latter is written more for patients than for health professionals and focuses strongly on antidepressants.

DTC marketing

New Zealand and the United States are the only countries where direct-to-consumer (DTC) print and television advertising of prescription-only medications is permitted, and both countries have allowed it, more or less, since about 1981. Whereas some of this advertising alerts consumers to a condition and simply bids them to "seek help" (advertises the problem), others actively promote individual products while making product safety or efficacy claims (advertises the solution).[86]

Pharmaceutical companies argue the practice enables patients to become actively involved in their own healthcare. Regulators argue that the enforced brevity of print and, especially, television advertising allows companies to omit important safety and efficacy information about the drugs and simply focus on their attributes. It is hard to police. Government regulators are more constrained by cost than drug advertisers: in 2010, for example, the pharmaceutical industry's budget for DTC advertising was approximately twice the budget of the entire FDA.[87]

The internet has become more than a bit-player in this story. For pharmaceutical companies, mental health providers and other related industries and government bodies, the internet provides opportunities to access potential patients, clients and customers in a way that appears direct and personal, but which can be handled as a mass-market, low-cost, easily-managed promotion. When Graber and Weckmann examined website information given by nine pharmaceutical companies, they found most of the companies came up on the first page (first ten links) of internet searches and that all of those company websites contained information that was advertorial and emotive. None of the company websites mentioned drug costs, only one offered efficacy statistics, adverse affects were minimized, and alternative drugs or types of therapy received minimal mention if any, making it difficult for consumers or doctors to compare drugs or make educated treatment choices based on company website information[88].

Furthermore, not all advertorial material appears on company websites. Unbranded websites[89] can be funded and supported by pharmaceutical providers without sponsorship disclosure; bloggers and opinion leaders can also be encouraged to endorse products online without sponsorship disclosure; and social media like Facebook and Twitter allow not only the originating source to share messages, but for ordinary folks to pass on those messages—with or without intent to advertise—without any sponsorship disclosure whatsoever[90]. In short, the internet provides an outstanding platform for unregulated pharmaceutical marketing on a global basis.

Part I summary:

The first four chapters of this book have provided a brief overview of mental health treatment up to this point in time. There are plenty of books and articles that go into far more depth and with attention to many issues that I have barely touched on, issues like medications for the elderly, the development and treatment of Alzheimer's disease, the role that insurance companies play in treatment (and the economics of treatment), the role of government bodies like the FDA, problems with the various medications, and so on. I have mentioned a few of the books that I think are of particular interest in passing, and I'll list them again here, along with others that readers might find enlightening.

Recommended books

Robert Whitaker's *Mad in America* and *Anatomy of an Epidemic* explore mental illness and psychiatric treatment (and their ramifications) primarily within the US. Whitaker is an investigative journalist; both of these books are well researched and compellingly written.

Toxic Psychiatry; Medication Madness; and *Psychiatric Drug Withdrawal: A Guide for Researchers, Therapists, Patients and Their Families* are just three of several noteworthy books by New York psychiatrist Dr Peter Breggin. The first, published in 1991, explores the dangers and damage caused by modern psychiatric treatment; little has changed in the 20 years since the book was written.

In *Medication Madness*, published in 2008, the author shares various case studies where psychopharmaceuticals have led to psychosis, criminal acts, violence, and suicide. *Psychiatric Drug Withdrawal* (2013) was recommended earlier in this chapter.

In *Let them Eat Prozac; Mania: A Short History of Bipolar Disorder;* and his latest book *Pharmageddon*, UK psychiatrist Dr David Healy explores the unhealthy relationship between the pharmaceutical industry and regulators, and examines the evolving nature of psychiatric diagnosis and treatment.

Crazy Like Us: The Globalization of the American Psyche by Ethan Watters looks at how American concepts of mental illness have been exported to Asia and Africa for economic gain.

Why the history matters

From my point of view, perhaps the most important thing to take out of the history of the treatment of mental illness in the Western World up until now is this: Before the 1950s, the mentally ill were generally perceived as abnormal and needful of separation from the rest of society for the good of society. Many mental patients were treated not as normal folks struggling with mental distress but as sub-normal humans, best isolated and constrained with chains or straight jackets and subjected to bleedings and poisons, cold baths, spinning tables, electric shocks, organ removals, deliberate brain damage, and disabling drugs, not to mention being forced to live in distressing conditions and often deprived of basic human rights and freedoms. There were glimpses of sunshine, of course: the moral treatment offered by the Quakers in the 1800s and the talk therapies developed by Freud, Jung and

Adler for those who had the time and money to pay for them. But for the most part, by any modern standards, the mentally ill endured distressing and demeaning treatments that were not notably helpful in restoration of equanimity.

From about 1950, the focus changed. Rather than the mentally ill being perceived as a liability and burden upon society, they were recognized as a seriously profitable consumer asset base for burgeoning chemical (pharmaceutical) companies looking to make and sell products. And once that market was saturated at the hospital and institutional level, it was expanded into the general populace to target the worried well, the aging, the sad, the disruptive, and the children. Ordinary life events have been transposed into fodder for giant corporations looking to make a buck--a case in point: the new DSM-V published in 2013 includes a diagnosis of major depression for anyone found still grieving two weeks after the death of a loved one[91]. Grief extending beyond two weeks, according to this well-respected guide, is an inappropriate psychological aberration that needs to be fixed.

In short (and I may be verging on heretical in suggesting this so bluntly): prior to around 1950, the general response to the mentally ill was to separate and contain them, and post 1950, the general response to the mentally ill has been to exploit them for financial gain. This is the world we live in today.

If someone wrote a science fiction book about a brave new world in which 20% of the population were taking mind-altering drugs prescribed by their doctors to ensure they met some documented criteria of "normal," even if the drugs didn't make them "normal," it probably would be tossed off as b-grade sci fi nonsense. Except, that's the state of psychiatric care in the industrialized West at the moment, and all the time, expansion is afoot to take these "diseases" and profits into new markets[92].

Spoon Boy: Do not try and bend the spoon. That's impossible. Instead...only try to realize the truth.

Neo: What truth?

Spoon Boy: There is no spoon.

Neo: There is no spoon?

Spoon Boy: Then you'll see. It is not the spoon that bends, it is only yourself.

--from the movie *The Matrix*

Part II

ॐ

Perspectives

Chapter 5: Assumptions & Presumptions
ଓଽଡ

Shortly after I completed my master's degree in psychology in 2011 at Victoria University, I signed up for Richard Bolstad's NLP practitioner training and subsequent master practitioner course[93]. I felt like I had come home. Here were people who understood the world the way I understand the world, and how we, as human beings, operate within it.

(If this seems like a curious diversion from what you've read so far in this book, bear with me.)

NLP stands for Neuro-Linguistic Programming, which originated in the 1970s when John Grindler and Richard Bandler studied the language patterns and techniques used by some of the world's leading therapists at the time and developed a model for understanding how people think and communicate.

There are several fundamental presuppositions for understanding the world and ourselves within the NLP perspective, but two in particular encompass a world view that is insightful and useful.

The map is not the territory

The first of these NLP presuppositions is *the map is not the territory*. That's a metaphor, of course, but imagine for a moment that you are a cartographer mapping a new territory for the first time. As you notice things in your environment, as things come to your attention, you add them to your map and try to make some inferences about the general lay of the land and how various elements relate to each other.

If someone else were mapping this same landscape, they would notice some different things, and would record them on their map in a different way, giving greater importance perhaps to one thing, and not even noticing another.

In real life, everyone has a "map" of how they think the world is. The important thing to remember is that it is only a map, not reality itself. Each of us has our own unique map(s) which we have developed ourselves, over time, based on our own, personal experiences of the world.

Other people have different maps. This is a really important idea. Other people do not see, interpret, and understand the world exactly the same way that you do. What's more, nobody has the ultimate reality map, and nobody's map is entirely "right" or entirely "wrong" or more "real" than anyone else's map. They're all just maps.

Maps are useful for understanding and interpreting and navigating around and through the various events and circumstances we encounter in our lives, but they are only as useful as we have been able to make them. More about this later.

Life, mind and body are integrated systems

Another basic NLP concept is that your whole life runs as a system, and is part of many systems. You have certain thought processes, particular patterns of behaviour, social interactions, work requirements, physical assets and limitations—all set within a body, a home, and a community environment, and within a governmental structure and environment that continually impacts the choices you make.

Your body is a system buzzing with activity: breath coming in and out, blood flowing, cells forming, cells dying, chemicals flowing, muscles tightening, muscles loosening, all happening as you sleep, eat, think, work, play, and move.

Your mind is another system, having developed a variety of processes for receiving, interpreting and reacting to real-time information coming in from outside your body as well as from memory storage and creative function. Notice that although your mind seems to be run by or through your brain for the most part, your mind is not your brain. It is informational and emotional content separate and different from the physical structures that allow that information to be collected, stored, manipulated, and used.

When something changes in your life, in your way of thinking, or in your body, the other systems are impacted. One could consider all of this one, big, massive mega-system that constitutes "you."

In understanding the psychiatric drug story, it is useful to recognize what happens from several perspectives—maps, if you will.

The drug researcher's map

Researchers who develop drugs are scientists. They get truly excited about coming up with ideas (hypotheses) and trying them out to see if they work. Whether testing new compounds in flasks and flagons or on rats, rabbits or "test subjects" (sometimes called "participants," less often called "patients," rarely called "people," and almost never identified as "individuals" with real names and personal lives known to the researcher), they are curious to see what will happen when their drug is trialled. It is an important part of the scientific process that researchers stay emotionally removed from their test subjects if their results are to have any recognized scientific validity.

A fundamental belief underlying this process is that a substance taken and a person's body/brain will combine to produce a particular and predictable reaction, just as two reagents in a test tube will respond a particular way when combined together. This belief is based totally on two assumptions: firstly, that mental distress is a predictable chemical and biological condition, rather than the result of environmental or situational events, and secondly, that a response in one individual is repeatable in another individual.

Furthermore, most scientists are specialists who hone in on particular aspects of a subject or process and often choose to exclude information they consider "extraneous".

When I was a psychology student at university, I took a course called *Drugs, Brain and Behaviour*. At one point the professor—eminent in her field—was talking about how a particular psychotropic drug affected the behaviour of rats in a certain study. I asked if that behaviour could be attributed to the way the drug might affect the rats' digestive system, and I was informed, that as far as this study was concerned, anything that occurred from the neck down was irrelevant to results.

A similar rat/drug story (that comes to mind as I write this) challenged the prevalent view that many drugs are inherently highly addictive, a thesis proven, apparently, by how laboratory rats are so eager to self-dose themselves. When Bruce K. Alexander and his colleagues challenged this belief by putting addicted rats—previously individually housed in tiny, barren isolation cages--into a "rat park" where they could socialize and play, the rats' drug use plummeted. Although their studies clearly demonstrated the role of social interaction and environment as factors affecting drug use and research, most other researchers dismissed their findings as of little significance.[94] After all, how can you control your experiment and your results if your rats are able to run around and do other stuff besides take drugs?

That sort of narrow focus—myopic some might call it—can prevent researchers from seeing a broader picture, but it represents what is accepted as a valid map of the world (how research is done and results are validated) for many researchers.

The marketer's perspective

Marketing departments of pharmaceutical companies have a very different goal in mind, and they operate with a different map of the world from researchers, although they may share the same desire to form a hypothesis and test it out in a situational setting.

The difference is, they have products that they want to sell, and the confirmation of success for their hypothesis is that they sell a lot of product and, ideally, make substantial profits for themselves or the company they work for. To do this, they need to make products as desirable as possible to as many people as possible. They get really excited when they can do that well.

There is a certain amount of creative fun in identifying or creating a need in the marketplace, creating an illusion of desirability with a product, and then testing the product in the marketplace to see how well it sells. A good marketer, as the old cliché goes, could sell refrigerators to Eskimos.

Whereas in past decades, pharmaceutical companies spent more on the research and development of products than on marketing, today the reverse is true with some $30 billion spent annually on drug marketing[95], more than the gross domestic product of most African and many Asian countries and island nations[96].

The directors of pharmaceutical corporations have a vested interest in making money. Indeed, by law they are required to put their shareholders' profits above the needs of their customers.

They too are playing a game with an element of fun—how much money can they make? How can they increase their profits? How can they pull a larger share of the existing market from their competitors? How can they expand the market and create new consumers? How can they ensure patients (consumers) continue to use their products long-term?

The doctor's perspective

Doctors generally have their patients' best interests at heart. They are also busy people with limited time to truly study the pros and cons, ins and outs, ups and downs of the drugs they prescribe. They know that when patients come to them with a problem, they are looking for a solution. The patient may be allocated 20 minutes for the entire appointment, barely enough time for brief greetings and pleasantries, for the patient to briefly share why s/he has come to see the doctor, for the doctor to make an assessment of the problem and give some advice and then write a prescription or make a referral as might be appropriate, and then for the doctor to write up a few notes for his own or the clinic's records. Some doctors work with 15 minute appointments, and allocate even less time for each patient.

Drug companies know that doctors are pressed for time, and want to follow "best practice"—the method or treatment that is standard and appropriate for the condition and the patient's needs. They are keen to have their own drugs part of recommended "best practice" care, and are also keen to have doctors encourage patients to use their products. To do this, they often send around pharmaceutical sales representatives (aka "drug reps") to introduce doctors to new products, methods, and applications, often with free samples for patients and copies of supportive literature. Other ways to encourage doctors to consider their products for treatment include promotions in medical journals, advertorials, symposiums and training sessions, information on websites, and journal articles.

Medical journal articles are often "ghostwritten" by writers from public relations firms hired by the pharmaceutical companies who are able to put a positive spin on data, even if it is unfavourable; the published papers are then officially "authored" by some well-known and willing academics or authorities who often have had little to do with the actual research or write-up of the results[97].

Although doctors themselves rarely if ever use the drugs or products they prescribe, they are in the very powerful position of recommending and promoting those treatments to/for their patients. Most doctors do so with the very best of intentions, but often without taking (or having) the time—and their time IS precious—to research the drugs, the background stories of the drugs, drug interactions, or the condition itself, let alone the specific underlying needs of their patients. And to go against "best practice" guidelines without clear justification can open up doctors to liability issues should something go wrong.

It's also important to remember than unlike most medical conditions where blood tests or urinalyses can be used to check for relevant factors, with mental illness there are no biological markers. A doctor must make a mental health assessment based solely on what a patient tells him and, perhaps, what he may observe about the patient.

To make this easier, there are several quick questionnaires—some even developed by pharmaceutical companies (they have a vested financial interest in an illness diagnosis)—that are commonly used by doctors to assess mood and mental stability. Most are 5-12 questions long and ask the patient to rate statements like "I have difficulty making decisions," and "I feel that life isn't worth living" on a scale of, say 1-to-5 where 1 is "never" and 5 is "all of the time". The patient's answers are likely to influence the doctor's treatment recommendations.

What about the patient?

Although the researcher, the marketer, the pharmaceutical CEOs and the doctors may find an element of fun and excitement, or at least a sense of satisfaction, in what they do, there probably isn't so much fun in this game for the patient caught in the distress of not feeling "normal". Although as individuals we like to think the *raison d'être* for the psycho-medical system is to help support us when we are struggling with life's issues, the truth would seem to suggest quite the opposite. Pharmaceutical companies cannot prosper unless they maintain and grow their consumer markets. Their success depends upon patients' distress, and it is the patients who support the industry, not the other way around.

The idea of taking a pill to fix your problems—or finding a medical solution for that annoying someone you live or work with (think teachers trying to work with hyperactive kids in a classroom)—is enticing. Pills are not only quick and easy to take, but they are relatively cheap to manufacture, prescribe, and administer. And most of us trust our doctors to make sound medical decisions for us; we assume they have the education, experience, and facts needed to do so. It's also comforting to hand our problems over to an expert to solve, kind of like giving the car over to the garage mechanic to fix that annoying knock.

Unfortunately, many people prescribed psychiatric drugs find the experience disappointing. Medications seldom do exactly what we want them to do, side effects can be onerous, and the prognosis for long-term users is not positive. Prescribers often tell patients on psychiatric medication that they will need to take the drugs "for life," a belief that is reinforced by the withdrawal response, often interpreted as a "relapse" that is enough to prove to some folks that they really need their pills, even if the withdrawal symptoms materialize as patently different from those of the original pre-drug problem that led to the initial prescription. Mental health care is chronic. Once caught on the psychiatric medication merry-go-round, it can be difficult to get off.

The focus of the industry is not really on the needs of the patient. Once a person becomes a patient—for indeed, as soon as someone hands responsibility for their healthcare over to the medical establishment they become patients—s/he often becomes less a focus of care and more a consumer of product, even if that person's emotional response is appropriate for their situation and likely to pass with time, such as a period of depression following the loss of a loved one.

Placebo

To determine if a particular drug is effective for a particular ailment, researchers compare how patients respond to the drug compared to if they receive no treatment. Since many people feel better if they know they are being treated (and the researcher will be looking for signs of improvement in treated patients, even if the patient herself may not notice a significant difference), trials are usually done "blind". This means that all participants enrolled in the trail are given identical-looking medication in exactly the same way, but one group of participants is given the actual drug, and the other is given an inert substance, euphemistically called a "sugar pill" (although placebos rarely consist of sugar).

In a blind trial, neither the participants nor the researchers monitoring the participants know who is getting the real medication and who is getting the placebo. However, it is often fairly obvious who has received the drug as most psychiatric drugs produce a range of side effects that may include nausea, headache, agitation, sleepiness or insomnia, etc., as well as changes in mood, thoughts and/or behaviours. To counteract this, sometimes an "active" placebo is used that causes minor side effects. To qualify for FDA approval, clinical trials must demonstrate the drug is more effective than a placebo for treating a condition. Drug companies do not, however, have to show that a drug is more effective than other drugs on the market, that it has a safer side effect profile than other drugs, or that it results in an improved quality of life[98].

In his book *The Emperor's New Drugs*, author Irving Kirsch explored the role of placebo in published antidepressant trials. He found that in 78% of clinical trials where active placebos were used, no difference was found between responses to the actual drug and the placebo response. And 82% of the responses to medication also occurred in the placebo groups. Furthermore, the greater the experience of side effects, the more "helpful" the drug was perceived to be, with a .96 correlation-- just short of 100%.[99]

Because a high placebo response makes a drug appear less effective in a trial, drug companies sometimes counteract it by doing a "pre-trial" where all individuals are given a placebo, and those who respond to it are eliminated from the "actual" trial with the drug.

It's easy to toss off the placebo response as *"just"* a placebo response but actually, this is a remarkable and important capability of the human mind to influence the body. Think of this in another way: in the antidepressant medication example mentioned above, over 80% of patients improved just by thinking they might be taking a helpful medication.

Of course some of these patients might have improved anyway—50 years ago before the advent of pharmacological treatment, depression was considered a self-resolving condition. Nathan Kline, mentioned earlier as a developer of the MAOI antidepressants and one of the tricyclic antidepressants observed, "Most depressions terminate in spontaneous remissions...regardless of what one does."[100] (Incidentally, no one in the pharmaceutical industry promotes that idea today.) And it's also likely that the simple attention generated by being involved in a clinical trial may be responsible for the improvement noted by some participants taking a placebo in a depression trial. Nevertheless, the ability of the mind to influence one's health is often unrecognized and almost always under-appreciated.

Chapter 6: Psychiatric Dis-eases
CR80

Coming back to the NLP idea "the map is not the territory," it's easy to see how a biomedical causation for mental illness seems to dominate our understanding and treatment of mental distress today. Yet the fact that there are no biological tests for mental illness, and the fact that an increase in psychiatric prescribing has not resulted in better mental health, statistically speaking, suggests this may not be a useful map.

This chapter examines specific common mental dis-eases—I like to hyphenate the word because I think it more clearly shows what we're talking about: dis – ease, as in "lack of ease", from Old French "without ease"—from an NLP and psychology perspective. NLP assumes a mind-body connection, and many New Age thinkers and some NLPers take this further to include spirit with mind and body. In any case, what you think, how you think, what you believe, how you perceive and interpret the world, and how you allow your body to respond to your thoughts: this all impacts on your mental health as you—or others—might define it.

And it IS important to understand that mental health is mostly a matter of perception moderated by society's definitions of "normal." Homosexuality, for example, was considered a mental disorder until it was removed from the DSM in 1973, while premenstrual dysphoric disorder (fancy words for PMS) wasn't considered a mental illness until it first appeared in the DSM-V published in 2013-- although an earlier version of the condition, late luteal phase dysphoric disorder (how's that for a mouthful?), was listed in the DSM-IV 1993 revision. (And let's be honest: most of us outside the psychiatric community would hesitate to consider this a mental disorder.)

Furthermore, our modern western culture has turned mental dis-ease into an incredibly powerful and wealthy mega-industry by perpetuating the idea that your problems are bio-chemical maladaptations that can be fixed through chemical manipulation.

There are times, of course, when psychiatric drug interventions are useful, expedient, and sometimes even life-saving. I believe these situations are relatively rare. I believe that for those of us who suffer from those everyday slings and arrows of outrageous fortune, learning to understand what we do that makes us suffer, and how to change those things we do, can make a huge difference. And for those things we cannot change, learning to see those things from a different perspective can be transformative.

Anxiety and depression

Anxiety and depression are probably the two most common mental dis-eases, and although it is possible to feel anxious without feeling depressed, or to feel depressed without feeling anxious, these two mood disorders frequently co-exist. That's probably because they share some common characteristics in thinking style and belief/assumptions, although depression is often backward-looking and self-deprecating ("I wish I had done x" or "I should have known better"), while anxiety is usually forward looking ("what if I do x and this thing I don't want happens?"), an apprehension that may be based on similar past experiences.

Physical symptoms of anxiety and depression can include back pain, chest pain, heart palpitations, headaches, feelings of suffocation, muscle tension, digestive disturbances, insomnia, and muscle spasms, while mental symptoms might include irritability, trouble concentrating, restlessness, worry, a feeling of apprehension or dread, avoidance behaviours, and concern about physical illness[101].

Probably the most important idea that comes from NLP about anxiety and depression is that these are not something you GET, these are something you DO. Unlike measles or chicken pox or malaria, depression and anxiety are not caused by viruses or bacterial onslaughts that invade your body. You learn how to "do" depression and anxiety over time, probably because of certain beliefs that you have.

Sometimes, of course, depression and/or anxiety can be chemically caused by drugs or withdrawal from drugs, including antidepressants, and it is important to take that possibility into consideration. I also suspect that various environmental contaminants, including exposure to electro-magnetic radiation (wifi, cell phones, microwaves), can increase levels of anxiety or depression, although scientific investigation of this phenomenon is still in its infancy[102].

Ultimately, we are all affected by our environment and the people within that environment so, for example, a child or adult who is being bullied at school or in the workplace or at home is understandably in a position where problems with anxiety or depression can easily develop.

Although it is useful and important to consider how outside influences may be exacerbating feelings of anxiety or depression and moderate those factors wherever possible, the following information about what you "do" to create depression and anxiety is still absolutely valid. It is easy to get caught up in a belief that depression and anxiety are inevitable in certain circumstances, but there are people in apparently hopeless or life-threatening situations who nevertheless do not experience significant bouts of anxiety or depression, and who remain cheerily optimistic in the direst of circumstances.

Let's briefly look at depression because it is common and something we can all relate to. Most of us—perhaps all of us—have experienced feeling blue. In most cases, we know why we feel blue, and we trust the feeling will pass, and it does. While many people have a seemingly innate ability to shrug off blue moods and just carry on, others struggle to pull themselves back to normal. Can we learn something from those who are good at soldiering on? A first step comes in understanding what defines depression.

According to the DSM[103], a major depressive episode or disorder is defined as having a depressed mood and/or loss of interest in life activities for at least two weeks, and having at least five of the following symptoms:

1) Depressed mood most of the day
2) Diminished interest or pleasure in all or most activities
3) Significant unintentional weight gain or loss
4) Insomnia or sleeping too much
5) Agitation or motor retardation
6) Fatigue or loss of energy
7) Feelings of worthlessness or guilt
8) Diminished ability to think or concentrate or indecisiveness
9) Thoughts of death

And for dysthymic disorder (think chronic rather than acute depression), the individual must have experienced a depressed mood most of the day, for more days than not, for at least two years, and be functionally impaired by at least two of the following:

1) Poor appetite or overeating

2) Insomnia or sleeping too much
3) Low energy or fatigue
4) Low self-esteem
5) Poor concentration
6) Feelings of hopelessness

The information needed to make a clinical diagnosis of depression is, of course, totally subjective. The patient is asked some questions, or responds to a questionnaire, and a diagnosis is made based on those responses given at that specific time. There are no blood tests, urine tests, brain scans or other physical diagnostic tools that can reveal whether a person "has" depression or not. So what's going on here? Why do some people allow themselves to fall into a black hole, so to speak, and what are they doing that allows them to sustain that depression for an extended period of time?

It is interesting to note that less than a hundred years ago, Sigmund Freud observed that melancholy—depression—generally resolved of itself, even without treatment, and suggested it plays an important role in ego development. He argued that melancholia could best be understood and treated through talk therapy. And you might recall medical researcher Nathan Kline's observation, quoted in the last chapter, "most depressions terminate in spontaneous remissions...regardless of what one does."[104]

New Zealand NLP practitioner Des Shinnick has developed a nifty process he calls "Rapid Depression Treatment"[105] where basically he teaches clients how to "do" and "not do" depression over the course of a couple of hours. Most of what he does involves body posture and attention, and it's quite insightful to be led through that process to discover what you already instinctively know: that sitting or standing or walking all hunched over with a downward, inward focus naturally makes you feel less open, less engaged with the world, and more likely to ruminate on things that are bothering you—standard symptoms of "depression".

By contrast, sitting, standing, and walking erect while taking in the world around you, smiling and laughing, looking ahead or up, and interacting with others makes you less likely to focus and ruminate on the things that bother you. You know the old saying, "Fake it 'til you make it?" Well, a good first step for anyone feeling depressed is to notice what they're doing with their body and how they are responding to their social environment and take remedial action. Your body and your mind work together, so if you address what one of these is doing, the other one will cooperate.

Try it: Sit or stand straight, look up towards the ceiling or sky, raise your eyebrows, smile, and try to think "I am so depressed." It doesn't work, right? Your body is not wired to be depressed when you take this position.

Obviously, though, there is more going on with depression than just how you sit or stand, or where you look.

A lot of what creates a feeling of depression comes with how you perceive and interpret the world around you--your mind map. There are three things that people tend to do when they are depressing:

1) When people are feeling depressed, they tend to focus on the past rather than on the future. It's a world of regrets and lost opportunities, often justified by a belief that it is important to learn from the past so as to not make the same mistakes in the future, or by a comparison of how things are now (perceived as "bad") compared to how they used to be

(perceived as "good"), or how they "should" be.

2) They tend to generalise from specific situations to tar a whole group of similar people, situations, or examples with a single brush: e.g., "*everybody* around here is useless," "*nobody* listens to me" or "I can't do *anything* right" or "I have *no* options" or "I just don't see *any* end to this situation".

3) They tend to associate into the particular problem (or problems), and feel like they are really caught up in the middle of a morass, allowing themselves to steep in the emotion and make that emotion feel bigger and stronger and more powerful, make it feel more "real" (and thereby more justifiable) even though that emotion is something they are creating themselves and it doesn't exist anywhere outside their body/mind.

There's a specific strategy that people often use to create depression. The NLP folks give us a neat little formula to describe the general strategy people use when faced with a problem. They call it the TOTE strategy. TOTE is an acronym for Trigger → Operation → Test → Exit.

Let me give a simple example of a TOTE: I want to print something, and I notice my printer is out of paper (Problem/Trigger). So I get some paper out of the cupboard and put it in the printer (Operation). I push "print" on the computer (Test), and if the document prints out okay, my problem is solved (Exit).

Many problems we generate don't have simple physical solutions like this one, often because they're tangled up with emotions. What often happens with depression is, something bothers us (Trigger), and then we tell ourselves it shouldn't bother us

(Operation), then we check to see if telling ourselves off for being bothered helped (Test), and it hasn't (failed the Test), so we tell ourselves off again, only harder this time (Operation), and it just goes around and around and around as a cycle without an Exit. Clearly, in this case the operation hasn't generated a solution, but if you believe it SHOULD solve the problem, or you don't know of a better strategy, you are often tempted to just keep doing the same thing, and expecting different results if you try harder.

A simpler and perhaps an even more insightful model of thinking strategy comes from psychological researcher and co-founder of the positive psychology movement Martin Seligman. In his book *Learned Optimism*, Seligman identifies a pattern of thinking that he calls the ABCs—A for adversity, B for belief, and C for consequences. According to Seligman, when we experience some adverse event, we interpret it through our beliefs, and we get certain consequences.

For example, you might text a friend and get no answer (adverse event); if you believe the person is deliberately not replying because she's cross with you, you might feel hurt (consequence) and counter that hurt by getting angry (reaction). If the belief portion of this process is altered, the consequences and reaction will be altered. If you think your friend probably left her phone at home (belief), you might be irritated with her (consequences), but you might just shrug and say, "Well, that's what Julie is like," and let it go (reaction). Same trigger, different belief, difference consequences.

Another significant difference between these two scenarios is in one you take on the blame/fault yourself (I've done something to make Julie cross with me) and in the second you ascribe the blame to someone else (Julie left her phone at home AGAIN—she's so forgetful!). Seligman research shows that optimists are less likely to blame themselves for problems that occur than pessimists, and this is especially true if that blame involves some personal character fault, e.g. "I'm just hopeless".

What's interesting is you probably know cognitively that you can sort of forget about the problem of feeling sad, or at least defuse it, if you focus your attention on something else (a strategy for resolving similar problems that you've probably found useful before), but you don't necessarily feel good about doing that. Why not?

Let's consider an example. Let's say you have recently suffered a relationship loss—someone you cared about has left your life. And you might have this underlying, seemingly-instinctive belief that if you don't continue to feel sad and distressed about that loss, maybe you didn't care about him or her as much as you should have. If you carry that belief, that your sadness and grief is a measure of how much you care, distracting yourself with other thoughts or activities or social interactions may feel like a betrayal of that person. And this ties in with how you perceive yourself as a person as well, as someone whose love is honest, pure, long-lasting and well-intentioned, certainly not someone who would betray a loved one. With that underlying belief, the distraction strategy—no matter how well it might work—is hijacked.

Of course, it is fairly easy to see how this works in an imagined scenario like this, but it is often harder to recognize when it is YOUR problem and YOUR underlying beliefs that support it.

Seligman had done a good deal of research on optimism and pessimism, and his work demonstrates that optimists are less likely to struggle with stress or depression, they have a lower cardio risk, and they enjoy longer life spans than pessimists do.

Pessimists and optimists think about and interpret events differently. If an event is positive, optimists consider that positive element to be permanent or long-term, pervasive and personal, while pessimists do not. A negative event will be perceived by an optimist as not permanent, not pervasive, and not personal while conversely, the pessimist will interpret that negative event as permanent, pervasive and personal.

As Seligman's book *Learned Optimism* suggests, however, people can LEARN to be optimists. And this is great news if depression and anxiety are your bugaboos, and you feel ready to change the underlying beliefs that fuel your habitual responses.

The power of the senses

The third thing that people often do when they are depressing (notice I'm using a VERB here, rather than the noun "depression," just as a reminder that depression is something you do, not something you get) is to magnify the emotions they are feeling, a skill also utilized to great effect by folks who are skilled in creating anxiety. When we think about things, especially things with some emotional attachment, we do so using our physical senses.

You might "see" something in your mind's eye, or "hear" the way something sounds. You probably have a feeling that goes with what you are thinking about, and you may have a little internal voice that talks to you or that you talk to (think, "What do you tell yourself about this?") or you may hear the voice of someone else telling you what you should be thinking or doing. There may even be smells or tastes or other sensations that you are aware of as a part of this story/memory/visualisation/projection that you are creating. In general, the more vivid these characteristics are that go with your story, the stronger will be the power of that story over you.

You've probably also noticed the word "story" that I am using here. I do use the term loosely, but it is a good reminder that whatever you are focussing your attention on is a story that you are telling yourself (and perhaps others), no matter how absolutely "real" or "true" it might seem to you. It may be based on something you've created and stored in your memory from the past, or something that you are actively creating now as a new story of the present, or as a story that acts as a projection into the future. The more vivid you can make the characteristics of that story, the stronger it will become and the more true it will seem.

Try this: Imagine lying on a beach somewhere in the tropics. You can FEEL the heat of the sun on your body and the rough texture of warm sand on your bare feet, grainy between your toes. You can SEE the blue sky and fluffy white clouds above you, and the turquoise blue sea near the shore, showing darker blue out over the reef and beyond to deep water. You can HEAR the sound of the breeze rattling and sighing in the palm fronds over your head, and the lap and gentle splash of the water on sandy beach as small waves roll in. You can SMELL the coconut scent of suntan lotion on your skin, and TASTE the ice cold tropical pineapple you are eating. That smiling INTERNAL VOICE in your head says, "It couldn't get any better than this!" I've given a positive example here, but we all do this sort of thing with negative stories too, even ones that haven't occurred but we think they might.

Now there are two ways you might do this. If you literally imagine yourself there on the beach like you're really there right now, we'd say that you are "associating in" to the story. If instead, you sort of "see" yourself there on the beach as if you are watching a movie, we say you are "dissociated from" the story. It perhaps isn't too surprising, that to associate in to a story is emotionally more powerful that to dissociate from a story. Interestingly, as your mind creates the story, your body responds to it.

To understand how this works, imagine you have a lemon, a fresh, bright yellow lemon. You take a knife and slice the lemon in half. It is so juicy, it squirts. You pick up a half of that lemon and tip your head back, hold the lemon over your mouth and squeeze. Drops of sweet-sour lemon juice hit your tongue. You lick at the cut face of the lemon. It's so incredibly sweet-sour-juicy your mouth tingles.

Now...come back to here and now and notice how you have more saliva in your mouth than you did before you thought about the lemon and tasting its sweet-sour tanginess. There is no lemon here. You only imagined it. But your BODY responded as if there was a real lemon here when you thought about it. That's the extraordinary power of the connection between your mind and your body. As you think, as you imagine, so your body reacts, preparing itself for what is to come.

So in the case of depression or anxiety, what often happens is we think about, we imagine, we make up a story about how things are, or we predict how things might be in the future. We get caught up in that story. And our bodies respond to what we think by preparing. If what we are thinking is threatening in any way, our bodies automatically swing into defence mode.

The autonomic nervous system

You've no doubt heard of the fight-flight response. Basically this means that when an organism—and we can include people here—feels threatened, its whole body automatically prepares to deal with the perceived danger by fighting or running away. Sometimes they call this the fight-flight-freeze response because there is, of course, a third option: to freeze in position (maybe the dangerous thing won't notice me if I stay very still).

The whole biological system that makes up your body has this automatic response to a perceived threat. It's a really useful rapid response when you are being threatened by a tiger, have to slam on your brakes, or some big dude has you cornered in a dark alley. It's not so useful when your body's nervous system becomes stuck in the fight-flight-freeze mode on a regular basis.

Biologists call the fight-flight-freeze mode the sympathetic nervous response. The opposite, and the mode you should be in most of the time, is called the parasympathetic nervous response—that's your rest-digest mode. I like to think of these modes as being "open" and "closed". Open, the parasympathetic response, is when your body is relaxed, your heartbeat is regular, your pulse rate is slowed, the bronchi in your lungs are relaxed, your blood pressure is down, your digestive system is working optimally, and basically you are just "chilled out," open and accepting to your environment.

What I think of as a "closed" response, the fight-flight-freeze mode or sympathetic nervous response, occurs when you feel threatened. To prepare for this threat, your body tenses up ready for action while normal, everyday functions closes down; your heart beat speeds up and may become irregular, your blood pressure increases, the bronchi in your lungs dilate, your liver secretes extra glucose, your digestive system shuts down, your pupils dilate, your blood vessels constrict, the adrenal glands on your kidneys secrete adrenalin (epinephrine), your sweat glands activate—and your body prepares to fight or run, or stay very, very still.

Fear

Depression and anxiety often come down to a fear response. Psychiatrist Elisabeth Kubler Ross, author of *On Death and Dying*, once said, "There are only two emotions: love and fear. All positive emotions come from love, all negative emotions from fear. From love flows happiness, contentment, peace and joy. From fear comes anger, hate, anxiety and guilt."

The idea that depression and anxiety can come down to one singular emotion, fear, is a challenging idea. As human beings and as a part of our culture, we have a vested interest in not being fearful. Fear is, of course, a really useful emotion in the presence of genuine, life-threatening danger, and no one suggests that fear is a surprising or inappropriate response for someone confronted with a menacing man waving a machete, an angry bear, or a diagnosis of brain cancer. Some folks even court this feeling of living life on the edge, hence the popularity of roller coasters, bungee jumping, climbing mountains, and hanging suspended in a shark cage surrounded by great whites. But fearfulness that lingers impairs our health and wellbeing.

The fear that can materialize as anxiety or depression is much more subtle than being afraid of sharks or bears or heights. Often, it is tied in, not with some particular and isolated physical threat, but as a longer-term situation or belief that lingers. It may be based around a perceived lack of security at a basic level such as not having enough money to pay the bills or buy the groceries, health challenges that impair the ability to continue what you normally do, or a loss---or risk of loss—of financial or social stability, or of a loved one. Or it can stem from an unconscious belief that a person is inadequate in some way (e.g., not thin enough, smart enough, strong enough, attractive enough, brave enough, well enough). And that is often solidified as a part of a person's belief system and self-image on an unconscious level.

Emotional priming

In her provocatively-titled book *Molecules of Emotion*, neuroscientist Candace Pert explored a long-running debate between psychologists: does emotion occur as a bodily reaction before the brain takes over, or does the brain govern emotional response? It turns out, it's both.

When something threatening happens and we launch into that fast-track emotional response that enables us to make split-second decisions, it seems like our automatic emotional system is clearly operating before our brain has had time to think. And in a way, this is so—that autonomic emotional system IS faster than cognitive thinking. But there's a catch. We respond the way we do because we have been *primed* to respond that way by thinking.

Priming is basically how your body/mind is prepared for a particular response because of previous experiences or information gained at an earlier time. Perhaps the most famous original example of priming as a scientific study comes from the Russian physiologist Ivan Pavlov who, in the early 1900s, discovered that if a bell or buzzer was sounded prior to feeding the dogs in his laboratory, the dogs would begin salivating just upon hearing the sound even if food was not forthcoming. Pavlov called this *conditioning*. It's like the little "try this" lemon experiment mentioned earlier in this chapter—all it takes is a trigger to spark the thought that sparks the bodily reaction.

It's been a long time since Pavlov's experiments, and psychologists have done some interesting studies with priming since then. Basically, priming makes you more sensitive to particular aspects of upcoming stimuli. Malcolm Gladwell, author of the popular book *Blink*, talks about one study where students were given a list of words and asked to make sentences out of them, and then they were observed or given an unrelated task to see if simply working with those words affected their behaviour.

After working with a list of words associated with old age and infirmity, for example, students left the room walking significantly more slowly than when they had walked into the room, and after working with a list of words on the theme of politeness, students were markedly more polite when given a task (to interrupt a conversation) than students who had been given different words.

In another study on priming, a Yale university study, PhD student Lawrence Williams showed how the simple difference of holding a cold drink versus holding a hot drink affected the way study participants felt about a particular individual they were introduced to. Participants who held a hot drink formed a more positive impression of the person than participants who held a cold drink. [106] It's hard to believe that something so simple, and so subtle, and operating so far below a level of consciousness as to be (you would think) totally negligible, nevertheless impacts a person's thought processes and social interactions.

Perhaps one of the most amazing demonstrations of priming was put together by British illusionist Derren Brown when he whisked two advertising gurus from the agency Saatchi and Saatchi by car to a secret location and asked them to quickly throw together some ideas for an ad campaign for a new taxidermy company. Before they started brainstorming, Brown left an unopened folder with his prediction of what they might come up with in the room with them.

The folder remained untouched during the 20 minute brainstorming session, yet the two ad men did, indeed, come up with concepts and wordings that uncannily mirrored Brown's prediction. The "trick"? Most of what the ad men brainstormed had been prompted by things they'd seen during the car ride to the study location[107]. The point is, your reactions to events do not "come out of nowhere."

Furthermore, your responses are not universally automatic. They are primed by *your* previous events and experiences, things people have said to *you, your* environment, *your* beliefs, and *your* value system. That's why, for example, one person may harbour an intense fear and revulsion of snakes while another approaches snakes with fascination, appreciation, veneration, and perhaps even love.

In his book *When Everything Changes, Change Everything*, Neale Donald Walsch reminds us that the emotions you feel may be *triggered* by exterior events, but they are *produced* by something inside you: "It's your ideas and your memories and your projections and your apprehensions and your understandings and your desires and your conditioning and more. And all of these things fall into one broad category. Thoughts. Thoughts sponsor all emotions."

Walsch further suggests that if we accept the general assumption that we are subject to automatic emotional reactions and must use cognitive thinking, thoughts, and will-power to overcome these emotional responses we don't want *after* they have occurred, then we have created a built-in handicap. But when we understand that our thoughts (ideas, beliefs, values, "truths") come *before* our emotional reactions, then we know that if we change our thoughts, beliefs, and values related to something, we can alter undesirable emotional responses before they happen.

So, where does this leave us with depression and anxiety? And don't forget that bundle of related diagnoses the DSM has gifted us with including post-traumatic stress disorder (PTSD), social anxiety disorder, panic disorder (with or without agoraphobia— that is, fear of being in public when having a panic attack), various specific phobia disorders, acute stress disorder, obsessive-compulsive disorder, and a variety of disorders recognized as being caused by medical conditions or drugs.

In Part III of this book we will look at some of the ways it is possible to change the thoughts and beliefs that keep us from living the life we want.

Bipolar

I haven't included bipolar disorder within the above section on depression and anxiety, even though it is generally considered a mood disorder, for a reason. The mania part of bipolar (remember, this "condition" used to be called manic-depressive) can lift individuals into the realm of psychosis—loosely defined as losing contact with reality.

According to the DSM, a bipolar diagnosis[108] required that not only the symptoms of depression occur, but that periods of depression alternate with periods of mania or hypomania (hypo means "under" or "beneath", thus someone who is hypomanic is not quite manic). Mania and hypomania are characterised by moods that are elevated, expansive, and/or irritable. Three or more of the following symptoms, according to the DSM, are needed to define a manic episode:

1) Increased self-esteem or grandiosity
2) Decreased need for sleep
3) More talkative than usual

4) Flight of ideas or the subjective experience that thoughts are racing
5) Easily distracted
6) Increase in goal-related activity or psychomotor agitation
7) Excessive involvement in pleasurable but risky behaviour such as unrestrained buying sprees, sexual indiscretion, or speculative investing

The symptoms of hypomania may reveal in a positive way by enabling an individual to accomplish amazing things: the ability to take risks, focus on goals, and sleep less can result in remarkable spurts of creativity, business success, and audacious behaviour that can charm and amaze others and bring considerable admiration, profit, and fame, a point clinical psychologist John Gartner makes in his controversial book *The Hypomanic Edge*. The problem occurs if these activities all go terribly pear-shaped, if the mild hypomania flares into full-blown mania, or when the bipolar sufferer crashes from high-function euphoria to a suicidal depression in a matter of weeks, days or sometimes even hours.

Psychosis

In addition to the mania element of bipolar disorder, psychosis is also a common characteristic of schizophrenia. Like mood disorders, psychosis occurs on a continuum that may range from someone who is mildly delusional about some particular thing but otherwise perfectly functional, to someone who has so completely lost the plot that they can no longer function in a normal situation. Extreme psychosis is disturbing not only to the person experiencing it but also to others as it often results in abnormal behaviours and reactions that are unpredictable.

The DSM offers a variety of specific disorders for diagnosis within the general category of psychosis. These include schizophrenia, delusional disorders, and schizoaffective disorder, and most of these have sub-categories of diagnosis, thus we have delusional disorder jealous type, delusional disorder erotomanic type, delusional disorder persecutory type, and so on. In the end, these are all just labels and as such, have as much value as you want to give them.

In terms of general characteristics, during a psychotic episode, individuals may experience a variety of symptoms including hallucinations, delusions, disorganized speech, disorganized behaviour or catatonia, and/or "negative symptoms" such as affective flattening. For a DSM-based diagnosis of schizophrenia, the guide stipulates that two or more of these symptoms must be present for a significant portion of time during a month.[109]

Hallucinations—being aware of something that others are not aware of—may involve any of the senses. Hearing voices[110] that seem to come from outside the body/mind is probably the most common hallucination, and these voices can be particularly distressing when they incorporate derogatory comments or preoccupying themes.

Not all hallucinatory voice experiences are negative or particularly intrusive, however, and many people who hear voices keep the experience from intruding upon their otherwise normal lives. An estimated 75% of patients diagnosed as schizophrenic experience auditory hallucinations. It is also quite common for people without any diagnosed mental illness to occasionally perceive voices that seem to come from elsewhere, especially during the hypnagogic state that occurs just when falling asleep or waking up.[111]

Visual hallucinations are less common than auditory ones as a factor of mental dis-ease, and can be caused by a variety of conditions besides psychosis including brain anomalies, tumours, drugs and drug withdrawal, alcohol and alcohol withdrawal, vision impairments, migraine headaches, and dementia. They can vary from visual disturbances such as lights, auras, colours, or zig-zag "interference" patterns to actual-size images of people, animals, insects, or objects.[112]

A delusion is a strongly-held belief that remains unsupported by hard evidence, is not generally accepted by others within the community or culture, and cannot be scientifically verified. Examples of delusions that may be interpreted as indicative of mental illness might include a belief that some other person or being is controlling your thoughts, that you are being stalked or monitored, that you are a god or have been specifically chosen by God to represent him/her here on earth, that you do not exist or are actually dead, or that some trivial remark or event has some great and highly significant personal meaning. Like any symptom, delusions can occur along a wide continuum that ranges from quite insignificant to debilitating. Not walking under a ladder because of a belief it will bring bad luck may be a delusion, but it is a relatively harmless one; believing that your wife or husband is actually an imposter (an example of the Capgras delusion[113]) is likely to impact upon your life and the lives of those around you in a pretty significant way.

Whether or not a belief is a delusion also depends upon the supporting culture and community. For example, a belief in God occurs for many as a fundamental precept within their particular social circle, and that belief remains unchallenged even though science has been unable to offer incontrovertible scientific evidence of God's existence. For others, a belief in God—because it can't be scientifically proven—is a delusion.

Disorganised speech or behaviour, another symptom of schizophrenia, is when these simply don't make sense within a normal context. When asked, "How are you today?" if the reply is something like "Dad tried to swing my eyes with a bike."—that's disorganized speech (although, as will be seen in the next section, there is a sort of logic embedded in a reply such as this).

Disorganized behaviour may be evident from inappropriate dress, like someone wearing four layers of clothing in hot weather, or if someone displays inappropriately confrontational or sexually overt behaviours. Individuals with severely disorganized thoughts and behaviour may not be able to care for themselves.

A flat aspect, not uncommon with diagnosed schizophrenia, is an impaired emotional response that may occur not only with personal emotions, but also in the recognition of emotional states of others. It often coincides with a slowing and dulling of the voice. Although generally considered a symptom of schizophrenia, this impaired response is also a side effect of the antipsychotic drugs given to treat symptoms of psychosis.[114]

Catatonia refers to a loss of movement or speech, muscular rigidity, odd posturing or posing which may be held for long periods, speech that echoes what others say, or odd grimacing. Like a flat aspect, catatonia can also be an effect of the psychotic drugs prescribed to treat the condition. Sometimes it's hard to separate the wheat from the chaff.

Psychosis from an NLP perspective

"It is a standard joke in psychiatry that neurotics build castles in the air, whereas psychotics actually live in them (and psychiatrists collect the rent)."
(NLP trainer Richard Bolstad)[115]

The DSM and psychiatric community allow us to recognize, classify and label different types and symptoms of psychosis, but don't explain what is actually going on. Besides "the map is not the territory" and "your life, mind, and body are interacting systems," the NLP model of the world also assumes

1) People make the best choices they can given their maps of the world
2) All behaviours have an appropriate and positive intention

With psychosis, individuals may find it difficult to clearly identify between "reality" and the metaphorical, sometimes dream-like version of "reality" that comes from their particular perception and interpretation of events and situations. Often they find it difficult to articulate their experience with "ordinary folks" who are unable to enter into their world. Yet there is an element of sanity in the world of the psychotic person, it's just happening on a different level. An example of this from Dr. Karl Whitaker, an American psychiatrist who focussed on family therapy:

In one first interview with a family with a schizophrenic girl, I turned to the girl after I'd been talking fairly emptily with the parents and asked, "What are you here for?"

She said, "Contact is good for colds."

I said, "How long have your parents been cold?"

And she said, "Twenty years."

We went on talking schizophrenese like this without any hesitation.[116]

This metaphorical way of regarding the world is known in NLP parlance as "chunking up" and "dissociating". To "do" psychosis, an individual needs to be very good at chunking up and dissociating.

Chunking up is a way of looking at something from a global or abstract or metaphorical perspective. To get an idea of how this works, consider a pine cone. Chunking up on the idea of a pine cone might take you to a pine tree, then to a forest, then to a forest ecosystem, and perhaps on to ecosystems in general. Or it might take you to seeds in general, then on to the origins of living things, perhaps to the origins of life itself, and perhaps even further on to the concept of God and what ideas God might be playing with in starting something "from seed". Or it could take you from a pine cone, to other small brown items with interesting textures, to textured brown items in general, to thoughts that, poetically, might be described as "like pine cones"—thus the pine cone and thoughts may be perceived as having a general kinship: both are brown (a mixture of contrasting colours), textured, and a part of "my" world. Chunking up allows connections to be made between objects and ideas that "normal" people wouldn't usually make.

On a metaphorical level, chunking up often occurs with stories or examples that carry a meaning beyond the obvious. When Morpheus in the film *The Matrix* offers Neo the red pill and the blue pill (see the quote at the beginning of Part I of this book), there is much more to the offer than just two different coloured pills. The blue pill metaphorically represents carrying on in the old way, unaware of the mechanisations that underlie our world (stay closed), while the red pill represents a willingness to be open to knowledge and awareness and truth over illusion. Indeed, the film is laden with such metaphors. Morpheus is the god of dreams in Roman poet Ovid's *Metamorphoses*, written some 2000 years ago, and Neo is a prefix derived from the Greek word *Neos*, meaning young, implying naïve and impressionable.

Poets are particularly good at chunking up in a metaphorical way:

> *Time let me play and be*
> *Golden in the mercy of his means,*
> *And green and golden I was huntsman and*
> *herdsman, the calves*
> *Sang to my horn, the foxes on the hills barked*
> *clear and cold,*
> *And the sabbath rang slowly*
> *In the pebbles of the holy streams.*
> (Dylan Thomas, from *Fern Hill*)

******

> *The shadows are empty, the sliding externals.*
> *The wind wanders around the house*
> *On its way to the back pasture.*
> *The cindery snow ticks over stubble.*
> *My dust longs for the invisible,*
> *I'm reminded to stay alive*
> *By the dry rasp of the recurring inane,*
> *The fine soot sifting through my south windows.*
> *It is hard to care about corners,*
> *And the sound of paper tearing.*
> (Theodore Roethke, from *Old Lady's Winter Words*)

Dissociation, another common characteristic of psychosis, involves the relationship of one's self with everything else. When dissociated, it is as if you view yourself and the events in your life as if from a vantage point outside of yourself, or as if you are watching yourself in a movie. This allows you to remain more emotionally objective and distant from a situation, which can be a really useful skill when confronted with a situation that triggers strong emotions.

Trouble occurs when one begins to confuse "out there" with "in here". One way this can manifest is with the voices that seem to originate from a source other than self.

Most of us have a way of talking to ourselves in our heads or thinking in words that in NLP lingo is called "auditory digital". Perhaps there are things you often say to yourself like "Come on, get this done" or "I can do this!" or "Ok, Stupid, figure this out!" or "Woo hoo!"—that's auditory digital stuff. It's also auditory digital when you plan or rehearse what you are going to say before you say it.

With psychosis, however, the auditory digital "feed" seems to occur without any conscious prompting or control, and is sometimes so powerful it's as if it were coming from—or being directed by— some force or being beyond the self. Sometimes the voice is of a recognized family member or associate.

The prevailing belief among psychiatrists and therapists is that these voices originate from within your brain—your subconscious or unconscious is talking to you. This makes a lot of sense and allows for the learning of a variety of strategies and skills to explore, understand, and "tame" the voices. But I'd be remiss if I did not at least raise the possibility, as food for thought, that in some cases at least, the voices might be real and external, and the rest of us just can't hear them. Perhaps the condition we call psychosis sometimes opens channels or access to realms or energy fields that are not detectible through everyday means.

In his book *Ultimate Journey*, consciousness researcher Robert Monroe talked about what he called the "M" field, which he defined as a "nonphysical energy field that permeates time-space" which he pointed out is not currently being studied nor, indeed, even recognized by modern science. He also talked about the "H" band, a "wave of disorganized human thought" that forms a part of the "M" field around Earth, and which astral travellers sometimes describe as like "a screaming, angry mob" to be passed through as quickly as possible.

That sounds pretty far-fetched, but it is not wildly dis-similar to the M-field postulated by British biologist and author Rupert Sheldrake. Sheldrake's M-field is a thought/energy field of morphic resonance that he believes underlies our mental activity and perceptions. We'll come back to this idea later in the book.

That aside, with psychosis, the "view" is often a big picture, abstract, vague, and distant. In many ways, it is like a profound trance state.[117]

A third problem that often occurs with psychosis is a lack of appropriate social skills. In the book *The Structure of Personality*, Richard Bolstad compares this sort of awkward social behaviour to the situation anyone might find themselves in if suddenly dropped into a completely foreign culture where the norms, values, beliefs, experiences, mannerisms, and ways of interpreting the world are significantly different from what we are used to. The inability to establish rapport with others, coupled with a lack of awareness of how to do so, or of the need to do so, makes it difficult for others to relate comfortably with someone who is psychotic.

Rather than assume psychosis is a biological problem in need of psychiatric medication (although that may be appropriate in some cases), the NLP viewpoint is that the psychotic person's map of the world has helped (or allowed) him/her to learn and employ skills that offer something of value. Sometimes these skills, thought mechanisms, and behaviours create a form of protection for the self, or an escape, or give a sense of general self-preservation. A person experiencing psychosis is responding in the way that seems for them most expedient for controlling a distressing or potentially distressing situation.

Since skills are learned, it is of course possible to learn new and different skills that might be more useful or more appropriate. Learning to "chunk down", for example, can come with an understanding of language use and patterns. Once you can name a pattern and identify how it functions, you can become more aware of its use in your own language and the language of others.

The founders of NLP, John Grinder and Richard Bandler, used the work of master hypnotherapist Milton Erickson and family psychotherapist Virginia Satir to catalogue a variety of language patterns that are commonly referred to in NLP as the "Meta model." By understanding how these patterns influence thinking and communication, and learning to challenge and alter the patterns, you can deliberately "chunk up" or "chunk down" language and thoughts.

For example, one common language (thought) pattern is mind reading, based on the assumption that you "know" what someone else thinks. "Jane knows I don't like making phone calls," Or "Mom will be cross if I'm late," are good examples. (To chunk down, ask "How specifically do you know?" or "Has there ever been a time when that wasn't true?")

Another pattern is the complex equivalent, which suggests that one thing means something else, thus "If we argue, the relationship is over" or "I already blew my diet today so I might as well eat the chocolate cake." On a metaphorical level—and like all metaphors this is quite sophisticated word play—Contact cold medication and contact between two people who are emotionally distant and therefore "cold" become complex equivalents.

One of the fundamental rules when using NLP for communication is to begin by "pacing" the other person, which basically means to create communication in a way that is reflective of how that person communicates. Most of us do this automatically in familiar situations: your conversation with a three-year-old is unlikely to be anything like your conversation with your lawyer, your best friend, or the woman at the check-out counter in the supermarket. Yet when one's thinking becomes disorganised, the ability to communicate effectively by altering and adapting to the needs of others seems to disappear. Thus, as Whitaker did in the above example, conversing with someone speaking (and probably thinking) in a (supposedly) disorganised way means meeting that person in his or her territory rather than expecting that person to meet you in your own comfort zone, linguistically speaking. It's more likely that a psychotic person with disorganized speech will respond "appropriately" when allowed to converse in his or her own language format.

Personality disorders

Also thrown into the mental disorder box by the DSM are a variety of personality disorders typified by certain traits that often negatively affect a person's life, especially as regards their relationships with others. These include traits that lead to obsessive-compulsive behaviours, avoidant and anti-social behaviours, dependent behaviours, paranoid behaviours, schizoid and schizotypal behaviours, narcissistic behaviours, and what is called borderline personality disorder. Often, other people are more bothered by these "conditions" than the person who "has" them because to that person they seem inherently normal, natural, and "just the way I am."

There are whole books written about these traits/conditions, and it's important to recognize that they aren't a yes, s/he has it versus no, s/he doesn't have it because these characteristics occur on a broad continuum. Many people that some might diagnose as having a personality disorder live quite ordinary—and sometimes extraordinary--lives. Also, these personality traits may tend to occur in certain situations, but not necessarily all of the time.

I briefly summarize the main personality disorders here:

- *Obsessive-compulsive disorder* is a type of anxiety disorder where a person attempts to thwart a perceived danger through elaborate or repetitive rituals such as repeatedly checking that a door is locked or by obsessive washing or cleaning.
- *Avoidant personality disorder* is a label given to describe a person with extreme social inhibition, people who fear humiliation, rejection, or ridicule from others and are likely to avoid social interactions because they find them extremely uncomfortable.
- *Anti-social traits can be* revealed as *psychopathy*—created from a combination of poor control of behaviour and anti-social behaviours that disregard the rights of others.

- *Dependent behaviours* are just that: when someone regards himself/herself as helpless and in need of support from others when there is no clear, physical need for that dependence.
- *Paranoid personality disorder* is hallmarked by ongoing suspicion and mistrust of others.
- The *schizoid* person isn't particularly interested in social relationships and prefers a solitary lifestyle. The *schizotypal personality type* takes this further by finding it difficult to correctly interpret social situations and offer appropriate responses. Others may regard him/her as "strange".
- The *narcissist* projects self-importance, power and influence which belie an underlying sense of inferiority, inadequacy, and low self-esteem.
- *Borderline personality disorder* is characterized by strong, unstable emotions and impulsive behaviours that often derail relationships with others.

All of the personality disorders can respond to therapy, provided an individual wants to make changes in his/her life by changing himself/herself. A really important idea from NLP is that you are responsible—"at cause"—for who you are and what you do. Creating changes in your life means doing things differently, and that's a scary proposition for many people. The way you've always done it is comfortable and familiar, whereas making changes can be challenging, and the results are unpredictable.

For many people with personality disorders, the familiar is more comfortable and secure than "being someone I'm not," and unless there is a strong personal desire for change, people with personality disorders rarely seek help. Those who live with people who have strong personality disorder traits might wish it were otherwise.

Understanding that formative events from childhood or early adulthood may be behind the development of many of these personality traits, and understanding that each of us is not only capable of learning new responses (you CAN teach an old dog new tricks, honest!), but DOES learn new responses all the time, albeit sometimes very slowly, means that none of these "disorders" is set in concrete.

General personality traits

While on the topic of personality disorders, it seems appropriate to look briefly at personality traits in general—not as "deviant" or "dis-ease" labels, but simply as a way to identify the foundations from which each of us operate.

The four "psychological types" identified below make up the Myers-Briggs type indicator, first published in 1962 and based on the work of Carl Jung. The Myers-Briggs questionnaire remains a popular "personality typing tool" often used by employers, educational institutions, and counsellors.

Most of us, for example, are familiar with the first psychological type concept of *introverts* and *extroverts*. Most of us enjoy spending time on our own some of the time, and being with others at other times. Strong introverts are more likely to feel most relaxed when by themselves or perhaps with one or two close friends or family members, while strong extroverts are more likely to relax when spending time with lots of other people. Extroverts look outwards and thrive through their social interactions and external environments, while introverts have a more introspective approach.

A second personality trait focuses on how you deal with information. A *sensor* tends to focus on immediate and practical facts and tends to be task- and goal-oriented, while an *intuitor* is more interested in the big picture, relationships, meanings, and ramifications that may be suggested by any given information.

A third personality dichotomy, the *thinker-feeler*, determines how you make choices and decisions. A thinker is logical, rational, and makes decisions cognitively, while a feeler trusts their gut- or heart-feeling, and is more in tune with values and instincts than with logic. Trial lawyers tend to be thinker-oriented: innocence or guilt is a matter of legal proof. A mother defending her child is more likely to follow her heart and gut instinct.

The *judger-perceiver* personality pair concerns whether you like things planned, organized, controlled, and predictable (judger) or whether you prefer a more flexible and spontaneous approach (perceiver). In scientific terms, a judger is "top down" (plan the experiment, then collect the data) while a perceiver is "bottom up" (collect the data, then figure out what it's telling you). In terms of a holiday, a judger prefers a planned vacation with a set itinerary and destination, while a perceiver might throw the tent into the car and head off for two weeks with no specific plans in mind.

There are several on-line questionnaires similar to the Myers-Briggs if you are interested in finding out about your own personality type, but note they each ask different questions in different ways so you may not get exactly the same results from one questionnaire to the next.[118] Also, results depend a lot on the context you are considering: a person might be fastidiously careful in his workplace, a party-hearty care-free soul on the weekends, and a loving and intuitive partner in the bedroom. So if you answer the questions as the "work you," you may get a different result from what you get when wearing your "home you" hat.

The NLP folks have added several other personality traits—what they call meta-programs—to this list which are also insightful to consider. One of my favourites, and a really useful one to be aware of, is the *matcher-mismatcher* meta-program. Matchers pay attention to similarities while mis-matchers pay attention to differences. In a conversation, for example, matchers tend to accept and agree with what you say (the sympathetic listener), while mismatchers tend to question and challenge your words and ideas (the arguer). Both skills are valuable in the appropriate context.

Another NLP personality meta-program, really a subset of the matcher/mismatcher meta-program, considers whether you move towards things you like or want, or away from things you don't like or want. For example, if asked "What do you want in a relationship?" a towards person will responds with a list of things they want; an away person will detail all of the things they don't want. You can see how a matcher would respond to the question as asked, while the mis-matcher would turn the question around and point out those things that are different to what s/he wants.

The natural inclination to chunk up or chunk down, skills mentioned earlier in the discussion on psychosis, and the inclination to associate into a "story", or dissociate from it, are also personality meta-programs.

ADHD

Attention Deficit Disorder (ADD) and Attention Deficit Hyperactivity Disorder (ADHD) did not officially exist until they appeared in the DSM-III in 1980, first as variants of a single disorder, and then revised from one disorder to two in 1987.

The latest DSM-V expands the diagnostic criteria to include adults as well as children which, according to the American Psychiatric Association, will "ensure that children with ADHD can continue to get care throughout their lives if needed."[119] I presume by "care" they are referring to (lifetime?) medication, and ensuring ongoing insurance coverage for disability treatment.

To be diagnosed with ADHD, a child (or adult) must show[120]

1) A persistent pattern of inattention and/or hyperactivity-impulsivity
2) Inattentive symptoms and/or hyperactivity must have first occurred before 7 years of age
3) Symptoms must occur in at least two settings (e.g., school and home)
4) Symptoms interfere with academic, social or occupational functioning
5) The symptoms cannot be attributed to any other disorder

To get an idea how these criteria are established, the criteria for inattentiveness (adequate to establish a psychiatric diagnosis) is that six or more of the following characteristics must be present for at least six months:

1) Often fails to pay attention to details, makes careless mistakes in school work
2) Often has difficulty keeping attention on tasks

3) Often does not listen when spoken to
4) Often fails to finish schoolwork or chores
5) Often has difficulty organizing tasks
6) Often shows reluctance to engage in tasks requiring mental effort
7) Often loses things
8) Often easily distracted
9) Often forgetful

When I read the above list, I am struck by how all of these characteristics—apparently description of a child whose behaviour is considered abnormal—are linked to classroom behaviour. Apparently, a quiet, compliant child who does what s/he is told (sensor, thinker, judger, matcher) is "normal", while a lively, curious, challenging, adventurous, independent, multi-tasking child (intuitor, feeler, perceiver, mis-matcher) runs a risk of being medicated to damp down those undesirable "symptoms".

I can personally appreciate the problem. I taught at intermediate and high schools for a number of years, and can instantly recall the "very challenging" grade 10 class I once taught that had four or five lads who were undoubtedly of ADHD type, mixed in with the 26 or 27 compliant students who genuinely wanted to learn the material, and I freely acknowledge the situation did not provide a satisfactory learning environment for anyone in the room.

I do not wish to get sideswiped here by the ancillary issue of how well our educational systems do (or do not) cater well for the marginalized student. I do think it is important, however, to recognize that while the medicating of difficult or disruptive children is a solution that can sometimes be helpful for a child, a child's peers, and his/her teachers and parents desirous of a more harmonious and conformist path forward at the time, it probably isn't treating a "real" psychiatric disease, and long-term drug use comes with complications that are probably not in the best interest of the child or the adult s/he will become.

Stimulant drugs like Ritalin and dexamphetamine, standard treatments for ADD and ADHD, increase heart rates and raise blood pressure. Common side effects reported by children and their parents include loss of appetite, sleep problems, and mood swings. A few patients experience psychotic episodes[121]. However, many parents, teachers and even children welcome the way the drugs enable the patient to conform to behavioural and learning expectations.

Worth a brief mention here is the idea of the indigo child. This New Age concept originated by psychic Nancy Ann Tappe in the 1970s suggested that some children born into this time of human development have particular abilities and characteristics that will help lead humanity into the future. Many of those characteristics parallel the symptoms of ADHD (intelligent, creative, easily bored, disliking systems and routine, often antisocial with others unlike themselves, sceptical of authority) leading some followers to suggest that ADHD symptoms are not a sign of mental malfunction but of evolution[122].

And so...

All of these personality traits and meta-programs that we have are constantly changing and adapting as we each evolve through our experiences as human beings. Some experiences and situations are best met with one kind of skill, while others are best approached in a different way. Disorders occur when we fall out of alignment with what our society has deemed "normal" behaviour for a given situation.

So what can we do about that? The next section of this book looks at how processes and tools for change can be used to bring dis-ease (as in, feeling without ease) to heel. Read on, Macduff, read on.[123]

Neo: What are you trying to tell me? That I can dodge bullets?

Morpheus: No, Neo. I'm trying to tell you that when you're ready, you won't have to.

--from the movie *The Matrix*

Part III
ᘓᗏᘔ

Tools for Change

Chapter 7: The Power of Awareness
ᘓᘗᘓ

You will, no doubt, recall the theories of the unconscious and subconscious suggested and developed by Mesmer, Charcot, Freud, and Jung mentioned a couple of chapters back. Although the modern scientific community prefers dealing with things that can be observed and measured, there is probably general agreement that the concepts of the conscious, subconscious, and unconscious mind are useful to describe how we perceive, learn, store, and use information, even if it's nearly impossible to quantify or qualify them.

A computer analogy

The modern computer gives us a useful analogy. On your screen, or available at the touch of your mouse or finger, you have all of the open files you are currently working with, and you can flip back and forth between them to access information, make adjustments, copy and paste, and change the "current event". This is all like the stuff you carry in your conscious mind. In the background, you have a whole lot of other files and processes that are stored away on the computer, not immediately in use but available should you want them. You are not thinking about them now, but you can access them if you need to. Think of that as the stuff in your subconscious.

Hidden behind that is a whole array of processes that occur as you play with the conscious and subconscious material: the operating system, the word processor, the organization and storage of data on the disc drive, the mechanical process of hitting keys and how that relays information to the operating system, and whatever else you may do to manipulate data. This gives you both opportunities to do things, and constraints on how things can be done that you might not even be aware of. That's like your unconscious.

As for Jung's collective unconscious, consider the internet—a vast compendium of information from uncountable sources, that you hardly know is there (and a whole lot of stuff that you really don't know is there), but which you can tap into on a regular basis for further exploration should you want to or need to.

That's not a perfect analogy, but it gives a pretty fair approximation. Basically your conscious mind contains whatever is currently in your present awareness. Your subconscious mind contains all that stuff that you're not currently aware of, but by simply shifting your attention, you can bring it up and put it on the consciousness table.

The unconscious mind manages a lot of stuff for you by rote: you can walk home or drive your car or pour yourself a glass of wine or breathe without consciously putting your attention on these activities because they have become habitual enough that they basically run on autopilot. You can choose to become consciously aware of some of these activities and processes if you want to, but it isn't necessary. The unconscious mind also contains material you cannot easily pull into conscious awareness but which influences the choices you make and the way you are.

The last part of the previous chapter that looked at personality traits and meta-programs suggests a way to make visible aspects of your unconscious patterning, although not necessarily the source of that patterning. Being an extrovert or introvert, for example, influences the choices you make in your careers, partners, and activities. Whether you are predominantly a judger or perceiver determines how you might approach a task or situation. Whether you are inclined to match or mismatch others will affect the way you perceive your environment and events, and will affect your social relationships. All of these meta-programs bubble along under the radar of your consciousness. And if you don't think about it, you may (inaccurately!) assume that other people perceive the world the same way you do.

How do people perceive the world?

> *What you see and what you hear depends a great deal on where you are standing. It also depends upon what sort of person you are.*
> --C. S. Lewis

Perception, as we usually think of it anyway, generally comes through the five senses: we see it, we hear it, we feel or touch it, we smell it, we taste it. Most of us assume that others perceive and remember things in the same way we do. Yet the NLP boffins remind us that most of us have favoured ways of perceiving the sensual information that comes to us, and favoured ways of remembering and accessing that information.

Probably the most common perception is visual. We "see" the stuff around us: our eyes are attracted by the beauty of a flower or a sunset or the flicker of light across a tv screen, we crane our necks to see what happened as we pass an automobile accident or watch a favoured athlete or team compete in a sporting contest. Most of us store visual memories too: how the house looked the last time you saw it, the colour of that dress, the "visual feast" set before us at a fancy restaurant: yes, even food—which you'd think would be predominantly tied to taste or smell—gets a strong visual treatment in most memories.

Other people are strongly auditory and are more likely to notice and store sounds to help create memories and emotional links: the chirping of birds, the sound and inflection of a voice, the roar of a plane taking off, a favourite song on the radio or a melody played on pan pipes in the Andes, the crunch of footsteps on gravel, the sound of gunfire.

The third most common sensory system is kinaesthetic, the sense of feeling or touch that comes with an experience. Not only is this a tactile sensation—the feel of a cat's fur or the vibration of an electric toothbrush—but it can also be the way you feel inside, within your body, as a response to external stimuli: the tension in your shoulders, a certain light-headedness, the urge to laugh, the knot in your stomach, or a sense of warm relaxation and perfect ease.

Smell and taste are less often dominant senses than the others, but they play important roles in certain situations or for certain people such as chefs or wine tasters. Most of us notice the smell and taste of a variety of foods: from the juicy lemon mentioned earlier in this book to hot, buttered popcorn to steak on the bar-be-que to sun-warmed blackberries picked off the bush to a hot cup of favourite tea. We notice the smell of a favourite perfume, cigarette smoke, wood smoke, farts, compost and roses—and our world is the richer for it.

Of course, much of the time we combine information gathered from all of these senses to form our impressions and store them. Thus a meal of Mexican steak fajitas may evoke the sight of red and green peppers and white onions and dark-grilled meat on a metal plate, the spicy smell of the meat and vegetables, the sizzle of a hot metal platter, the sensation of saliva rising in your mouth and the hungry hollowness in your stomach, and then the glorious taste of that first bite.

Memories are often triggered—sometimes unexpectedly—by some particular sensory experience: a certain perfume or cologne, for example, or a certain song, a particular shade of blue, the feel of rain on your face, or the thud of a sledgehammer.

The NLP folks have noticed that most of us favour a particular sensory method of accessing our subconscious information or memories, and we may use that same method or a different one for how we tend to represent the world to ourselves. That sounds complicated, but it isn't really. And it isn't hard to figure out which sense is dominant for you.

When accessing information from your memory bank, if you tend to instinctively look upwards to recall something, at least initially, you're more likely to be dominantly "visual." You also might be inclined to rub your eyes or forehead, gesture upwards, or lean forward as you recall memories. If you favour the visual mode when you talk about something—this is the "represent the world to ourselves" bit—you tend to use visual words or phrases like "I see what you mean," "It's just what I've been looking for," and "I just don't have a vision for it." Good spellers given an unusual word often look upwards as they visualize how that particular word looks. (The legions of primary school teachers who admonished, "Johnny, you won't find the answer on the ceiling," were not doing their young charges any favour.)

People who are strongly "auditory" tend to look left or right (towards the ears) when remembering something, and they may touch or gesture towards their ears, mouth, or chin. They hear what something sounds like, or words that describe it. Verbally, they may prefer to use hearing words and phrases like "It sounds good to me," "That rings true," and "These ideas are so discordant!"

Kinesthetically-inclined people tend to look down and to their right when recalling things, and may touch or gesture to parts of their body as they speak. In speaking, they are likely to use tactile or feeling phrases like "It just feels good," "I need some solid feedback," and "I wish I had more guts."

All of this is stuff that happens in the background at an unconscious level. And it's useful to know that you do that, and that we all have different ways of remembering and recalling information, and different ways of representing the world to ourselves. But for the moment, just store that idea away, and let's take a look at how one goes about making changes on a practical, conscious level. After all, we have more control over that, right?

Creating change on a conscious level

When people want to make changes in their lives, most start on the conscious level with the stuff they are immediately aware of. It often begins with the recognition of a problem, and the desire to diminish or eliminate that problem.

Life coaches help people identify changes they want to make and develop strategies for doing so. Of course, nobody needs a life coach to make changes, but understanding how this works can be helpful in making changes more quickly and easily than might be done if you just spend a lot of time thinking about how you wish your life were different.

So, first you need to identify what you want to achieve: your outcome. What is it you want? Many people coming from a place of mental discomfort might say "I want to be happy" or "I want to get rid of this depression" or "I want to stop feeling anxious" or "I want to have a better relationship with my partner (or kids or parents or siblings or co-workers)" or "I want to stop overeating (or smoking or drinking or being lazy)". You might notice that whereas statements like "I want to be happy" or "I want a better relationship..." are affirmative and allow space for someone to move forward in a positive direction, desired outcomes often come from a place of wanting to move away from something such as depression, anxiety, uncomfortable relationships or bad habits.

One of the problems with moving away from something is that the further you get from it, the less strong is your desire to avoid it, and that's true over both space and time. Furthermore, avoidance behaviour is generally linked with the emotion of fear, and fear as a motivator is not particularly compatible with mental health. So let's not go there. Moving towards something you want is almost always a stronger and more powerful motivator than moving away from something you don't want, and it is constantly renewable. So make it positive.

If your desired outcome is an avoidance one, see if you can flip it around and turn it into a positive goal worth striving for. For example, "I want to get rid of this depression" might become "I want to live my life with joy, appreciation and gratitude," or "I want to feel well and full of energy," or "I want to be enthused about my life," or "I want to be happy." If you're not sure how to turn it around, ask yourself this question: "If I didn't have this [thing I don't want], what would I have instead?" In NLP terms, this something we call reframing. More on that later.

Simply identifying how you wish to feel or be is a step in the right direction, but it's still pretty vague, fuzzy stuff. Sometimes when looking at ways to change things, we get caught up in the state versus goal conundrum, and it's important to understand the difference. A state is a vague mind-body-response (feeling) that comes from a particular situation or activity. A glass of wine can make you feel relaxed; a parking ticket can make you feel tense, anxious or angry. These are states, and they change all the time. Being "happy" or "depressed" are states as well. You can learn to change states by altering your perceptions, beliefs, responses, body position, focus of awareness, environment, or by taking action (you can call your lawyer, put on some music, talk to a friend, focus on your breathing), but it's highly unlikely you'll achieve it by simply setting a goal of "I want to be happy." If it were that easy, you would have done it ages ago.

Goals that you have decided to work towards, on the other hand, have measureable outcomes. These are things that may help you to alter undesirable states over time by helping you to change habitual responses, but they are not necessarily state-changers in themselves. Examples of goals might be "I will get more fit" or "I will get a job (or get a different job)" or "I will lead a more social life" or "I will make more money than I'm making now" or "I will learn to manage my unpredictable emotions." All of these goals can be reached by changes you can make in your life, by things you can physically do.

However, to really be successful and KNOW you are successful, you usually need to take this goal-setting to the next level and make your goal so clearly defined that you can measure the results. Set a benchmark and a deadline. So "I will get more fit" might become "I will run a half-marathon in six months". "I will make more money" might become, "I will make $60,000 in the next 12 months." It is important that those actions be realistically achievable through your own efforts: winning the lottery might change your life and solve your problems, but it is not a realistic goal to set because although you can buy a ticket, you have no control over the results.

If a goal is fairly long-term, like over several months or a year, it is useful to break it down into more manageable chunks. (Old joke: How do you eat an elephant? Answer: One bite at a time.) So decide what you are going to do *today*, and *this week*, to move closer to that goal. If you want to get fit, you might resolve to get out for a walk or run at least 30 minutes every day this week. If you want to get a new job, you might resolve to this week a) do some research on the internet; b) talk to a friend who works someplace you'd like to work; and c) update your old CV. If you want to deal with an anxiety problem you might decide to take up meditation, and set aside 10 minutes every morning this week to practice meditation.

But heads up: when one thing changes, it's likely that other things will change as well. It's important to be aware of the implications of changes you make in your life. Having an understanding of these "ecological" issues will help you make good choices and decisions ahead of time, and that can be useful. For example, if you decide to quit smoking, it's important to consider carefully how this will impact your life. Your health will improve, of course, and it's better for your family, and you'll save money—and that's all really good stuff. But smoking is also a social activity, so how will your social life be affected? Will you have to give up "going outside for a smoke" with your friends or colleagues? Are there other smokers in your home? If so, will that create friction or offer temptation? How easy will it be to break the cigarette after a meal or sex habit? How about weight gain? That familiar something-in-your-mouth habit, the fact that nicotine is an appetite suppressant, and the fact that food tastes better once you quit because your taste buds function properly again mean that when smokers quit, they often gain weight—are you okay with that or, if not, how will you deal with that? And nicotine-deprived smokers often experience extra anxiety and stress when they first quit—so how will you deal with that? None of this is to discourage anyone from quitting the smoking habit, but being forewarned is being forearmed.

Take time to brainstorm the many things you can do to help reach your goal, and identify the resources you already have to help you get there. These resources might include knowledge or access to knowledge sources, time, people, money, a sense of inner conviction and belief, a sense of humour, God's help, whatever—make a list or a "mind map" diagram and pin it up where you can look at it regularly as a reminder of the options and support that you have.

Re-evaluate your goal(s) on a regular basis, and make changes as you go along. If last week you did your job-hunting research, talked to a couple of friends, and polished up your CV, this week you might set a goal of applying for three jobs. If last week you spent 10 minutes every day meditating, but you're not sure if it did a lot of good to alleviate your anxiety, this week you might decide to track your anxiety level in a journal, and identify how pausing to breathe slowly in....out.... for three breaths every time you feel anxious affects your anxiety level, plus bump the meditation up to 15 minutes a day, and maybe try it with soothing music.

Lastly, give yourself a little reward when you hit your goals. At the very least, pat yourself on the back for doing today what you'd set as the day's goal, and perhaps a bigger "Woo hoo" when you complete the goal(s) for the week. Kids often respond to charts and earned stickers. It may sound silly, but lots of adults love to see those shiny daily stars accumulate on their goal chart too—so if you're a star-minded soul, buy yourself a packet of stickers, make a chart, and put it up on the fridge. It's a cheap and very visual record of your accomplishments. And splash out on a little something special when you hit a specific milestone—celebrate your achievement with a meal out, a glass of bubbly, an afternoon at the beach, or a bouquet of flowers.

Interlude—freeze frame

Setting aside the conscious/subconscious focus of this chapter for a short interlude, I'd like to talk a little about HeartMath[124] and a super little practice Doc Childre and his team have invented called Freeze Frame. When I put on my coaching hat and work with new clients, I almost always share this little gem in the first or second session, regardless of the issues or goals that may be the primary focus of our attention—it's that worthwhile.

I've mentioned a couple of times already about the idea of breathing to control anxiety. Since anxiety, and various other undesired emotional states like anger, frustration, irritation—stress in general, really—are common issues with almost all of us, knowing about and being able to use the Freeze Frame technique enables us to take control of our automatic negative reactions to a situation and defuse the emotion while responding to our own, innate wisdom.

When you are under stress, upset, anxious or angry, your heart beat becomes irregular, your brain stops functioning at its best, stress hormones like cortisol and adrenalin (norepinephrine) begin to cascade through your body, and your good health and well-being are compromised. Indeed, just a few minutes of anger or anxiety can impair your immune system for hours[125].

Back in 1999, Doc Childre, Howard Martin and Donna Beech published their oddly-titled book *Heart Math Solution*, the culmination of 30 years' research into heart intelligence and the power of emotion—especially stress—to affect physical health. In the book, the authors shared their discoveries about the brain-heart connection, and how working with the heart can bring harmony and health to the body and the mind.

The Freeze Frame technique is the first and simplest of the techniques they teach in the book and at their excellent website (see www.heartmath.org). It's a quick and easy way to restore equilibrium to your body while also giving yourself time to make intelligent choices when you're having one of those "blow out" moments, and it is so much better than being railroaded by gut reactions you may later regret.

You know how, when you're watching a DVD or pre-recorded television program, you can push the pause button and freeze the screen? And how doing so allows you to shift your attention from what you were watching to another task: going to the bathroom, answering the phone, checking the meal in the oven, or talking to someone else who might be watching the same program? And then you can go back to the program when you've dealt with those other things? Well, the freeze frame technique works a whole lot like that. Basically, you flick the emotional situation into freeze frame and give yourself time to decide how best to deal with it. It works like this:

Freeze Frame Step 1: Become aware of when you are feeling stressed. Many of us are so used to that stressed-out feeling, or have become so accepting of stress inevitability in our lives, that we have come to ignore the signals. Classic symptoms include tense muscles, an unsettled stomach or churning gut, a lump in the throat, an instinctive angry or tearful response—each of us has our own cues, and by the time they get to the point of physical manifestations, the stress is clearly out of control. Step 1 is to simply recognize a stressful situation when it occurs and notice how your body is responding to it. Then take a "time out" and go to step 2.

Freeze Frame Step 2: Shift your focus away from whatever has upset you and focus your attention on your heart instead. Imagine your breath is flowing through your heart-space, and slow your breathing down and breathe slowly through your heart-space for at least ten seconds. By focussing on your heart, you shift your attention away from the problem to possibilities for a solution, and you create a brief nurture-space for your mind and body at a distressing time, reminding your brain and heart to work together to resolve the problem.

Freeze Frame Step 3: Recall a time when you felt positive and at ease, perhaps a time you were visiting some place you love, or a time you were caring for a child or an animal, or a time you were spending with someone you love. Allow yourself to feel the way you felt then, full of peace and love and gratitude and joy. It's important that you pull up that *feeling* memory, not just recall a snapshot of yourself sitting on Waikiki beach.

For many people, step 3 is a bit difficult, so if it is hard to quickly think of a time when you felt that sort of warm-fuzzy-relaxed-grateful feeling, you might prepare for doing the freeze-frame by picking a happy memory *now* and practice pulling up that warm-and-safe, glad-to-be-alive feeling, rather than waiting to do so during a more challenging moment when you are in the middle of an anxiety crisis.

Freeze Frame Step 4: Now, while focussed on your heart and holding that warm, fuzzy, glad-to-be-alive feeling in your body, use your intuition and common sense and ask your heart what would be the best response you can make in this particular stressful situation. When you ask this question to and from the heart-space, you give yourself time and permission to listen to your own innate wisdom, or the wisdom of your higher self, if that concept resonates for you, and are more able to make insightful, intelligent choices that can not only defuse the current situation, but allow you to move into the future with more awareness, presence, peace, and tranquillity.

Freeze Frame Step 5: Listen to the response from your heart-space and respond to the situation accordingly. Sometimes the answer you get will simply seem like common sense; other times, you may find unexpected insight and wisdom.

When you first start to practice using the Freeze Frame, work with little things. Try to notice when you are simply irritated with something: when someone says something that bothers you, or when something you are trying to do isn't as easy or as quick as you'd anticipated. Try to make the "go to your heart" response your default reaction to any stressful situation.

Using the Freeze Frame technique may seem awkward at first, especially when you are interacting with others. Give it time, and you will soon discover how powerful this simple technique is when you use it regularly. If you are with people you know well, you might simply ask for two minutes of "time out" and go into another room or the bathroom to run through the process. After you've run the process enough times, it will become so instinctive, you can run it on the spot without seeming to significantly interrupt what you are doing. Practice makes perfect, so if it doesn't seem all that easy or profound the first couple of times you try it, give yourself permission to practice it daily, maybe several times a day, for a couple of weeks. And take advantage of even minor upsets for practice—every time you do it, it's good for your heart, and your mind.

At the heartmath website mentioned above, you'll find several other techniques like this one to lower stress levels and bring the head and heart into coherence; information and research on stress, heart health, and heart-mind coherence; and a number of tools for assessing or monitoring your stress level.

The Freeze Frame technique works on that interface between our conscious and unconscious minds. By noticing the stressful response we have to a disturbing situation or thought, noticing how that stress affects our body, and changing our initial "Oh no!" response to one that is more empowering, healthful, and wisely intuitive, we can take charge and change our body's reaction, our thought processes, and often the outcome of the precipitating event. Powerful stuff indeed!

The subconscious on autopilot

Why should we have to do this? It's easy to get sucked into an underlying belief that the conscious mind is more powerful than the subconscious, or into a belief that these two minds are at war with each other. Neither is true, of course. Both work perfectly well at what they do. The problem occurs when the automatic subconscious response is not what we *want* the response to be.

There are two ways that subconscious responses are commonly created. The first is by repetition. When you do something enough times, it creates a default mode that the subconscious can follow so well, your conscious mind no longer needs to think about it. I think of it as like a worn path, like might be created once enough walkers have trod down the path to the point they make a depression in the dirt. When you start down that path, it is easiest to follow the rut in the meadow rather than walk through the tall grass on the verge. Neuroscientists explain it as if each time a jump is made from a specific point on one neuron to a specific point on another neuron, it reinforces that particular route, making it more likely that this specific connection will become preferable over other options, all things being equal.

Take riding a bicycle. The first few times you rode a bike, when you were just learning, you had to think about what you were doing and train your body to respond to the movement of the machine: pedalling, steering, balancing, adjusting to speed and a sense of movement. At first, you wobbled and hesitated, but soon you could pedal up and down the street with confidence. Once you learned how to ride a bike, your subconscious could work with your body so efficiently that you could watch the scenery, avoid obstacles, be wary of traffic, and carry on a conversation while riding that bike and never once think about the actual bike-riding process. It's really quite amazing, when you think about it.

The other common way that subconscious responses can be created and seemingly set in concrete occurs when there is a strong emotion involved. You only have to be stung by a bee, bitten by a dog, or rejected by a lover once for an instinctive wariness to be created. Your subconscious mind, which is always on the alert for danger, is there to protect you, so it stores the information that a particular thing or activity is dangerous. That's why they always say, "When you fall off the horse, you need to get back on," and "once bitten, twice shy."

Many of our fear/avoidance patterns occur because we have been hurt—physically or emotionally—by another person. When we believe we deserve to have our needs met by someone else, and that person (or those people) lets us down, we often feel a sense of betrayal or a violation of our trust. While immediate emotions of disappointment, hurt, shame, anger, or worthlessness may be obvious and understandable at the time, and the conscious mind may understand that it was a one-off event that won't happen again, those strong negative emotions can leave a track in your subconscious.

When there is another interaction with that person, or a similar situation crops up, your subconscious flicks into autopilot and runs along that old track, reminding your body that there is a risk of harm or distress in this situation, based on previous experience, and that defences must be raised. Unfortunately, while the subconscious is very good at quick responses, it is not so good at discrimination, so even when an event or interaction is consciously perceived as a "safe" situation, the subconscious can continue to ring those alarm bells. And even when the conscious mind knows a situation is "safe," it is not very good at over-riding the subconscious mind.

Reframe

I have given everything I see in this room [on this street, from this window, in this place] all the meaning that it has for me.
--Lesson 2, *A Course in Miracles*

Something becomes a problem for us when we attach a particular meaning to it. We think in the context of "when *this* happens, it means *that*." When he turns his back on me, it means he doesn't like me. When she doesn't eat all the food on her plate, it means she doesn't like my cooking. When that driver cut in front of me like that, it meant the driver doesn't respect me enough to give me the courtesy (or safety margin) he should give me. In short, I am not valued.

Assumptions like this can, of course, be wrong. He may have turned his back to you because he was simply changing positions, he was distracted by something else that pulled his attention, or because he was thinking about something else. She might not eat all the food because she isn't hungry, or she is distracted, or she doesn't feel well, or she really hates beans. He might have cut in front of you because he was a bad driver, he'd been drinking, he was distracted, he was late for something he considered extremely urgent, he doesn't know any better--or any of a dozen other reasons.

We needn't—and probably shouldn't—take the actions of others personally and feel affronted every time they don't comply with our own idea of what is appropriate. Even if these assumptions might be true, is that a sufficient reason to get upset? And if so, how will our lives be made better by the process of getting upset?

In NLP, we talk about the concept of framing and reframing. If you've ever taken a painting into a frame shop and tried out different combinations of matts and frames, you know the outer presentation significantly affects the overall appearance of the painting and how you react to it.

In NLP terms, a frame is how you identify and interpret a specific scenario. Reframing is when you look at it another way. We frame and reframe all the time. You have an idea or belief and think that this is how something is (a frame), and then a new idea or piece of evidence comes along that adds to or contradicts what you "know." You can then choose to add that bit of new information to your picture and reframe it, or you can reject that new information and keep the old frame.

Consider this collection of possible frames about anxiety: When I feel anxious, it means there is something wrong with me. When I feel anxious, it means there is something wrong with the situation. When I feel anxious it is because somebody else did something that upsets me, and they shouldn't do that. When I feel anxious, it means I need to fix a problem. When I feel anxious it means I need to avoid a problem. When I feel anxious, it means I have an anxiety problem and that has nothing to do with me personally or with this particular situation or these particular people, it's just hormonal. When I feel anxious it means my inner intuitive wisdom is reminding me there is something I should be paying attention to. When I feel anxious I know it's time to go walk the dog. When I feel anxious, I need to have a drink to calm down. The drugs I take make me feel anxious, but I need to take those drugs.

Can you see how many different ways something can be framed? Can you see how we attribute meaning to something (in this case, anxiety) and think this attribution is the truth?

It's often hard to demolish an old frame and create a new one because we usually think about our problems the same way every time we think about them—it's the old "trot down the rutted path" routine. The challenge is to think of the problem from a different angle. If you are not working with a coach who can walk you through this process, one thing you can do is a little "problem analysis" and then brainstorm alternative frames.

So, think about a problem you have right now, and if you want to start addressing it right now, take the time to get out a piece of paper and a pen and write down answers to these questions: What are the symptoms of the problem? When do you do you it, or have it? Is it always there? Are you aware of it all the time? If it's not always there, then how do you know it is time to do or have this problem? When is the problem not there, or when is the problem less noticeable? What is different about those times?

Now ask yourself, what do I want? And why don't I have that now? If you remember the goal-setting exercise, you might recognize this as an ecology question. And this is a reframe too: What is the problem giving you that you need or want? Just as cigarettes can help a smoker create social bonds, calm nerves, and regulate food intake, something like depression can give you time on your own to think, an opportunity to generate sympathy from others, and/or an excuse to avoid doing something you don't want to do or be someone you don't want to be. Sometimes what we consciously don't want is a default mode the unconscious falls into because the default seems like the easiest pathway forward.

Next, think about the root cause of your problem. Sometimes this is hard to do because "thinking" implies a conscious process, and the root cause may be subconscious or unconscious. If you jump every time you hear a car backfire, and you recognize that is a holdover from time you spent in a war zone when the sound of gunshots indicated trouble or danger, then you know what the root cause is.

Often, though, the root cause is considerably more subtle than that. Often it is based on a limiting belief. A limiting belief is a belief that limits you. To suss out what limiting beliefs may be holding you back, think about the problem and consider your responses to these sentence starters:

I'm not...

I can't...

It's impossible to... (or, It's too hard to...)

I don't have enough...

S/he won't let me...

I'm too...

And sometimes it's based on a belief that you hold on to so strongly that it seems heretical to let it go, even though it makes you you feel anxious or angry even as you cling to that belief. Some examples of this might be that that other people should care about your wellbeing as much as you do, that other people experience the world the same way you do, that you need to be responsible for those who depend upon you, that if you work hard you will be rewarded for your effort, or that good things come to those who wait. I'm not suggesting that these ideas are right or wrong, but I am suggesting that they are beliefs—not hard-core scientific truths--that may underpin your thoughts, actions, and mood responses.

So, if you're playing the problem resolution game right now, take out a fresh sheet of paper and do the same thing I did with anxiety above. Write down as many meanings as you can for the problem or issue, whether or not you believe them to be true. Then, flip the problem around to see how it can become a resource or learning tool or asset. When you do this, you are reframing!

Notice how things like shifting the blame from yourself to others, or from others to yourself changes the frame. Notice how you can take a particular behaviour or situation that you assumed was a problem and turn it into an asset.

One of the great business examples of how reframing turned a problem into an asset occurred back in the 1960s when Hertz was the number one car rental company in America. Avis turned their second-place status into an asset by adopting the slogan "When you're only number 2, you try harder." Their "We try harder" slogan rocketed the company's market share up from 11% to 34% and the slogan remained in use for fifty years.

Notice how reframing allows you to look at old things in a new way. Even if you reject many of the meanings and frames you can brainstorm for your problem, it is likely that just thinking about these possibilities will change the way you regard the problem, resulting in a frame shift.

So far, this frame and reframe process has been mostly on the conscious level—you've used your conscious mind to raise your awareness of possible reframes of a problem. In the next section, we'll look at how you can use your subconscious mind to create powerful shifts in perspective.

Reframing depression

> *When your living conditions are stable, peaceful,*
> *and prosperous—no civil wars raging in your*
> *streets, no mass hunger, no epidemic disease, no*
> *vexation from poverty—making yourself miserable*
> *is a craft all its own, requiring imagination, vision,*
> *and ingenuity.*
> *--Cloe Madanes*

In a wonderful essay cheekily titled *The 14 Habits of Highly Miserable People*[126], therapist Cloe Madanes highlights effective strategies that depressed people use to become and stay miserable. She doesn't do this in a "mean" way, but it is a splendid illustration of how being miserable can earn you sympathy, help you avoid disappointment, and create a persona of yourself as a wise but tragic figure. I like how she's turned the tables on all those many books and articles with titles like *The X-Number of Habits of Highly Successful, Effective, Creative (etc.) people* to make the point that being miserable is a learned and learnable skill—a reframe from undesirable to desirable. And this is important because from an NLP perspective, *all behaviours have an appropriate and positive intention.*

So, according to Madanes, how do you "do" misery? I'll share a sampler with four of her tips here:

First, you need to worry about money, and not only your own precarious financial situation, but also the financial situation and cavalier attitude towards money expressed by family, friends, community, country, and even global economies. You may do this out of a genuine and sincere desire to see others avoid the traps you've fallen into, to remind yourself to learn from your own mistakes, to reassure yourself that you are not alone with your troubles, or because of a subconscious belief that worrying about a problem will in some way help to resolve it.

Second, you need to ruminate on how boring your life is and consider taking action to alleviate this situation (have an affair, go on a shopping spree, quit your job, start a fight).

Third, let your misery become part of your identity. Make sure everyone knows you are a Depressed Person, and focus your thoughts and conversations on that identity. Make it clear you don't want to be this way but you just can't help it— it's just the way you are and you are a product of how life has treated you. And maybe it's in your genes. You can't help that, right?

Fourth, expect the worst of others. Assume they have their own self-interest at heart and that they are out to humiliate, embarrass, or take advantage of you. That way, you can be pleasantly surprised if their words or actions are genuine or helpful, and you won't be disappointed if they live up to your negative expectations. Before any encounter, be sure to go over all of the ways that person has disappointed you in the past so you will be prepared for the worst.

In her essay, Madanes even suggests practical exercises to develop each of the "habits". When you see being miserable touted as a set of skills you can learn and hone, the reframe allows you to recognize a whole series of beliefs and behaviours that have helped you create your world.

Hypnosis

Basically, hypnosis can be defined as a relaxed state of focused mental attention that allows a willing participant to be susceptible to suggestion. It is most definitely not the same thing as sleep, although the word derives from the Greek word *hypnos* meaning sleep. Rather it is more like a meditative or trance state that, some hypnotherapists believe, allows access to the subconscious or unconscious mind. The word "trance" is somewhat controversial however, as American obstetrician and gynaecologist William Kroger observed: "It's not a 'trance'... That's the most ridiculous term for it. [Hypnosis] is a state of increased awareness."[127]

If I were to ask you to shut your eyes and remember a time when you were sitting outside in a park, and if I asked you for some details, you would be able to tell me what the weather was, the colour of the bench you were sitting on, whether or not there was a pond or stream, grass, birds, sun or shade, other people around, kids, dogs, bikes, ducks... And you could remember—and fill in with imagined details if you could not remember—what it was like to sit in that place at that time, perhaps to the point that if I asked you, "Where are you now?" you might answer "In the park." But your physical body would be, of course, somewhere else entirely. Your mind would have simply allowed you to journey to a place from your memory or in your imagination. And you would be in a state of hypnosis.

When you are in that sort of state, it is possible to influence your subconscious mind through the power of suggestion. While working with a hypnotherapist or NLP practitioner is a good way to find or create resolution of many problems that seem to have a mental origin, once you understand the process, you can create some changes yourself quite easily.

Lots of people have at least occasional trouble getting to sleep at night. When this happens to me, here is what I do. First I get myself into a comfortable position. Then I pay attention to my breathing for a several breaths, often counting slowly to 4 on the inhale, and exhaling slowly to a count of 8. Then I imagine all of the stuff that I'm thinking about as physical "stuff" and I imagine putting all of it into a box or basket and stuffing that box or basket into a closet to be opened back up tomorrow. I imagine shutting the closet door. Then I check my body for any points of discomfort or tension. If a spot feels tense, I tense it harder, hold it, then... relax... Snuggle down...I think about three or four things that I'm really grateful for, and smile. They don't have to be big things, just things as simple as a nice dinner, a sunny day, a call from my daughter, the comfort of the cat curled up at the foot of the bed, or a phone call from a good friend.

Next—you know the old hypnosis countdown? Well I do that in my head. I think, "I'm going to count down from ten, and as I count down, I will feel more and more relaxed and more sleepy until I fall asleep. So, at 10—I'm feeling very relaxed now (insert deep breath and slow sigh), this bed is so comfortable, these blankets are so cosy, the pillow cradles my head just right. Slip down to 9. I'm ready to go to sleep...now... My body feels so very relaxed and rather heavy, sinking gently into the mattress, my awareness is beginning to drift...drifting...now..and that's so nice...I'm feeling so sleepy and so relaxed...so relaxed..now...and...slipping down now through the layers of sleep to 8. Feeling heavy... tired... sleepy... breathing slowing... slowly... slow... drifting... time for dreams...time for healing of body and mind...time to just let be... And... dropping down to 7. Now. And deeper into sleep... deeper into comfort... even deeper into total relaxation, now... I notice the patterns of light visible behind closed eyelids...I'm watching the patterns... watching the patterns... watching... patterns... and slip down to Level 6..." And so on. Most of the time I don't get much below 6 before I'm out. I think of this approach to sleep as drifting down through the layers, and it works like a treat. You can also drop down through the layers by taking (in your mind) a long down escalator, perhaps through the floors of a large, multi-storey department store, or by walking down the stairs of a large and gracious building. You can explore the hallways, and open doors to dreamways...

Many therapists who use hypnosis in their work with clients often use a script something like this to put their clients into a relaxed state, although not with the specific purpose and wording to get them to actually fall asleep. Once in a very relaxed and dreamy state, suggestions can be made to the subconscious mind, sometimes through the use of imagery or stories or metaphors, that make it not only possible but quite easy for clients to let go of old patterns of thought or behaviour that no longer serve them, and/or establish new ones.

For example, if a client wants to get over a broken relationship, once s/he is in that relaxed and dreamy state, the therapist may ask them to *review the present time as if it is seen from a great calm distance, looking at the relationship now through time and space, or as if seen through a window or a lens, and it's soothing to create that space between what was a distressing time and the present you going into the future...and you are like everyone who can experience the flow of time and change and know the present at that time felt very real but now can be seen as distant and flowing and time and associations and experiences allow you to move on and change the things you were worried about at that time like clear water flowing gently over coloured pebbles and...*

I just give a little taste here. This is an Ericksonian[128] type of hypnosis "script", and you can see it doesn't make a lot of sense to the conscious mind at all, but the unconscious mind will take on board the concepts of distancing oneself from a troubling experience while accepting change and the passage of time as natural and desirable when those ideas are presented within that sort of dream-like framework. You might even notice how commas are left out to obscure clarity in what is being said: while the conscious mind is trying to figure out what this is all about, the unconscious mind is simply taking it all in. When presented within a therapeutic framework, a hypnosis session like this might be half an hour or longer, so this truly is "just a taste".

Hypnosis, and appeals to the subconscious and unconscious mind, need not involve therapy sessions if the mind is open. In the book *Monsters and Magical Sticks*, clinical psychologist and hypnotist Steven Heller shared the story that inspired the title. When Heller's son was three or four years old, he became firmly convinced that at night, his baseball and football became monsters, a situation that caused a great deal of angst for both the child and his parents, and often resulting in nightmares after the boy had finally had fallen asleep. His parents' attempts to explain and reason with their young son—appealing to his conscious mind—were frustratingly ineffective. Logic clearly wasn't going to work. The problem needed to be dealt with in the language of the problem.

Thinking outside the box, the boy's parents fabricated a magic wand with a bit of doweling, some purple velvet, and a golden tassel—and presented it to their son in a special gift box ostensibly from a magic doctor. They taught the boy some "magic words", and assured him that the magic doctor's special monster-banishing wand would ward off any threats from the monsters. When bedtime came, the young lad made a careful pass around the room with his new wand, diligently cleansing each corner of danger with the magic spell. The results were, indeed, magical. The nightmares that had so plagued the household ceased from that very night, and the need for the wand and magic words dissolved within a few days.

It might be easy to dismiss Heller's success with a small child, but the same kind of approach can work equally well with adults who are experiencing various degrees of "psychosis," (and I use the term very loosely) or who have belief systems or ways of thinking that are not a comfortable match for your own. Rather than flatly deny or argue with seemingly irrational beliefs, subjective experiences or peculiar responses, friends and family often find it enabling to enter into and accept that person's irrational belief system when spending time with that person— working "with" is almost always more productive than working "against".

You can also use this sort of approach yourself, imagining a particular process in a creative way. Individuals who are ill with cancer, for example, are often encouraged to get themselves into a meditative state and then visualize their body defences destroying the cancer cells and/or their affected organs as healthy and fully-functional. Results can range from gently empowering to downright miraculous. For more information on that, a worthwhile book is Dr. Bernie S. Siegel's *Love, Medicine & Miracles,* or check out Silva Mind Body Healing on the internet[129].

Not all people are susceptible to hypnosis presented in the "traditional" therapeutic (or entertainment) sense. I read somewhere about 10% cannot be hypnotized at all, and about 10% are very susceptible, and the rest of us are somewhere in the middle. And there may be some truth in that sort of ratio. But in reality, any time we allow ourselves to remember, dream, or imagine, we are creating a space of susceptibility. And any time a friend invites you out for a coffee or a beer, or asks you for a favour, your subconscious ensures you have some level of susceptibility to their suggestion. (And remember the priming example given earlier in this book where simply holding a warm drink made people think more positively of a new acquaintance than hold a cold drink did.) In that sense, all of us experience a basic hypnotic process on a fairly regular basis whether we recognize it or not.

Hypnosis is not a magic wand. It cannot change your exterior reality, at least not in the first instance. It CAN enable you to alter your framework, however, so you perceive and interpret your exterior reality differently, and in doing so it can enable you to make changes that are beneficial in many and various ways.

Time line

One hypnosis-related process that I like very much and that is very effective with clearing out old limiting beliefs or emotional "snags" that affect how you are today involves imagining a time line of your life. By imagining yourself floating high above that time line, stretching far into the past and far into the future, you can easily visit times in the past that have influenced your present life; clear out unhelpful emotions, decisions, or beliefs that were made in those past times; notice how events that come after those critical junctures are changed when the past emotions, decisions, or beliefs are changed; and recognize how altering emotions, decisions and beliefs that resulted from a past event can change your future.

I'm not giving specific directions for the process here, simply explaining briefly how it works. I suggest if this sounds like something you'd like to try, you should find a practitioner experienced with Time Line Therapy™ to walk you through the process a few times until it becomes familiar. After that, provided you aren't working with issues that are deeply disturbing, you can easily run the process yourself. If you do have significant issues from the past you wish to resolve in this way, working with an experienced therapist is a fantastic way to do so. Many NLP therapists have training and experience using Time Line or a similar process.

The time line process is one of several methods that allow for apparent influence from before a time of conscious memory in the currently life. Sometimes the source of a particular problem seems to come from the time of birth, the time spent in utero, a time before birth, a previous life, or an event or time in the life of a parent, grandparent or ancestor. Whether this is an actual subconscious memory or a metaphorical one doesn't matter—neither the therapist nor the client needs to believe in past lives or intergenerational memory for the process to be effective.

Just in passing, but on a related note, in her book *Remarkable Healings*, psychiatrist Shakuntala Modi shares her experience of many psychiatric patients experiencing profound healings through hypnotic exploration of past and past life traumas, births, and deaths.[130] Modi also shares examples of what she calls soul fragmentation, caused when a part or fragment of the Self seems to have ripped off from the whole and got caught in a sort of traumatic time warp—see the section on matrix reimprinting in the next chapter for a different but related exploration of this idea.

The time line process neatly incorporates resolution of past trauma and soul fragmentation issues without need for any sort of deep hypnosis trance-state, labels, or fanfare.

Brain waves

To understand a little bit better what goes on in your brain when you are awake and conscious, or during hypnosis and other states such as relaxation, meditation, and sleep, researchers have measured and studied the electrical impulses that move within the brain using an electroencephalograph (ECG). Their work has led them to label 5 frequency bands of electrical activity that occur in the brain, depending upon what a person is doing.

The most common frequency for the awake, conscious mind when doing general activities is called *beta*, and this has a frequency range roughly 14-25 hertz. This occurs when you are alert, active, thinking, and aware of your surroundings. As the intensity of mental processing increases, the hertz level goes up. By the time it reaches 30 Hz and higher, which it can do, the frequency is known as *gamma*, and this occurs when every part of the brain is needed to simultaneously and intensely process information—times of peak concentration.

Slower *alpha* waves occur between 8-14 Hz, and this seems to be a sort of "bridge" frequency between the conscious and unconscious mind. When it occurs, the mind remains alert but the conscious mind is not actually processing much information. This is the state of mind you pass through as you are just drifting off to sleep, or when engaged in light meditation, or intuitive thinking. Artists and musicians often operate (to an outsider, apparently consciously) at the "alpha" level. This is a very peaceful, relaxed, and healthy state of functioning. When inducing a hypnotic state, many therapists use a music soundtrack that emphasizes the slow rise and fall of the alpha state frequency.

Slower yet are *theta* waves, between 4-7 Hz, and here the subconscious mind is in full play. This is the brain's primary mode during dream sleep, deep meditation, or a deep trance. The theta mind is rich with imagery, fantasy, creativity, and intuition while remaining unfocussed and free of conscious restrictions. This is probably the time when the unconscious mind is best able to process, consolidate and integrate material from the conscious activities of the day.

Delta waves, slower than 3.5 Hz, are prevalent during deep, dreamless sleep and when the body is unconscious.

Our brains rarely operate in just one band or level at any given time, however. Our overall brain activity usually shows a mixture of frequencies, depending upon the area of the brain and the activities one is engaged in, and no one frequency is intrinsically better than another—it all depends upon the activity being pursued. Interestingly, and just as a side note, while deep meditation is usually associated with theta waves, long-time meditators also show a significant increase at the gamma frequency.[131]

Chapter 8: Energy & Emotion
ೞഩ

Luminous beings are we, not this crude matter.
--Yoda, from *Star Wars*

Traditional Western-trained biologists, psychologists, and medical practitioners see human beings not as energy systems, but as beings composed of physical matter that *use* energy, gained mostly through food, to enable their physical movement and thought processes.

The calorie is a scientific unit of measure for this energy, and it represents the amount of energy needed to raise the temperature of one gram of water one degree centigrade. Most people are more familiar with kilocalories—1000 calories, confusingly also called Calories, but sometimes written with a capital "C"—which are used to measure the energy the body receives through the metabolization of food. This focus on food for fuel to drive the body much like fuel can drive a car is a very mechanical approach to understanding the body and energy, an idea that is not only limited in scope, but which ignores a vast compendium of information from non-Western traditions about body energy.

This is, I think, unfortunate because so much of what goes on in our lives, both physically and emotionally, is energy based, and we're not talking here about the number of calories in your Big Mac. Our bodies are not simply organic mindless machines taking in food and expelling waste, but are intelligent ecosystems capable of self-correction and endowed with the ability to overcome dysfunction. Energy is a key factor. We generate, use and expel energy not only through physical means, but also through mental and emotional activities.

It seems to me that strong emotions are like powerful packets or bursts of energy that can leave traces and knots and tangles within us, while often exploding outwards towards others and into our environment. Although this is often good—there is nothing like heart-felt joy and laughter to raise spirits and enhance well-being, for both the generator and the receiver—a great deal of the distress and dis-ease we experience in our lives is caused by harmful bursts of negative emotional energy that we generate ourselves, or that we absorb—intentionally or not— from other people or our environment.

To begin to get a handle on this idea, this chapter looks briefly at two well-known body energy systems and ways they can be explored to enhance both physical and mental health. Mind and body, after all, are connected. I might even dare to suggest that mind and body are really just one single "ecosystem".

Qi

The ancient Chinese people used the word "qi" (sometimes spelled ch'i or chi) to describe life energy. They believed that qi came not only from food but also from the air, from parents (heredity), and from the universe. They believed (and still believe) that qi flows through the body along specific energy pathways called meridians, and that it is stored in energy centres in the body called dan tiens. The three main dan tiens are in the lower abdomen below the navel (Japanese people call this energy centre the hara), the heart centre, and the head or brain.

The Chinese have been working with qi energy for thousands of years. In ancient times yang sheng, (nourishing the forces of life) and tu gu na xin (expelling the old energy, drawing in the new) were practices probably derived from ancient shamanic animal dances. By the 6th century BC, a Taoist practice known as *dao-yin* advocated exercise-type movements, positions and breathing to cultivate qi and enhance healing and general health. Modern *t'ai chi* and *kung fu* clearly have roots in *dao-yin*. The term *qi gong* (working with life energy) first appeared in a text dated to the fourth century AD[132]. Today, *qi gong, t'ai chi*, and their many variations are popular practices throughout the world. While some people may enjoy these activities primarily as a physical and social exercise, others may develop their own private practice to cultivate increased personal awareness, health, and well-being.

Besides the three primary energy stores or *dan tiens*, smaller energy centres can be found along the body's energy meridians, and these are traditionally identified as useful points for applied acupuncture or acupressure. In traditional Chinese medicine, it is believed that health is created when the body's yin (passive) and yang (active) forces are kept balanced. They believe the insertion of tiny needles into these energy centres can enhance the energetic flow and balance when, for some reason, the acupuncture point has become blocked or the energy there has become stagnant, or there is some other energetic disruption. Activation of these points through pressure or massage, rather than needles, is also effective for relieving a variety of ailments. The art of massage developed co-currently with qi gong in ancient China.

Modern Western medicine has not been able to identify specific physical components of the body to account for the presence of the *dan tiens* or acupuncture points, although several theories have been advanced. There is enough evidence that acupuncture works, however, for it to be fairly widely accepted as a useful adjunctive therapy with Western allopathic treatment, and sometimes even on its own. Acupuncture can be particularly effective for pain relief, nausea, and muscle relaxation as well as being useful for increasing general immune function. On a mental health basis, numerous studies have found acupuncture at least as effective as antidepressants for depression and without any of the side effects that come with psychiatric medications.[133]

Prana and the chakras

The concepts of body energy, energy storage centres, and the movement of body energy along channels are not confined to China and Chinese tradition. In India, the Sanskrit word for life force energy is *prana*, and the origin of the concept, like that of *qi*, goes back into the ancient recesses of time. In India, the *dan tien*-like body energy centres are called *chakras* and are described as spinning wheels or vortexes of pranic energy contained more-or-less within the body. Written references to the *chakras* as centres of consciousness and energy occur in the Hindu *Upanishads* (philosophical texts, the earliest dating to circa 600 BC), and it seems likely that the concept itself pre-dates the written records. The energy from these wheels or vortices is said to travel through the body along channels called *nadis*, which were originally believed to centre in the heart.

The modern take on chakras identifies seven major energy centres in the body, usually depicted in a rainbow of colours beginning with the lowest (red) at about the level of the tailbone and pubic bone, and the highest (violet) at the top or crown of the head. In her excellent book *Energy Medicine*, author Dorothy Eden shares her understanding of the chakra system, and I have based some of the following information on her work.

According to Eden, each of the chakras is associated with certain organs and parts or aspects of the body as well as the endocrine system, emotions, personality, overall health, and an individual's personal, psychological and spiritual journeys. She believes each of the chakras has seven layers, with the top layer most related to current or recent events, and more fundamental elements of a person embedded in deeper layers. She also notes that the different layers of each chakra spin not only at different speeds, but can also spin in different directions.

The lowest or "root" chakra is most often associated with primal survival and belief, our basic instincts, our immune system, and the fight/flight/freeze response. The root chakra is also our "grounding" chakra—the concept of "root" is not just metaphorical—and it channels energy into all of the higher chakras from the earth. In the ancient *Upanishads* and yogic tradition, the root chakra is seen as the home of kundalini, the coiled snake of potential spiritual development that can be aroused in seekers of spiritual truth. Usually depicted in coloured diagrams as red, the root chakra can incorporate many other colours. Eden states this colour variability is true of all the chakras.

The second chakra is sometimes known as the sacral or womb chakra, and is the chakra of potential. Situated about two inches below the navel and depicted as orange on colour charts, this chakra governs not only the sexual organs but also the intestines and bladder, the organs that pull the last of the nutrition from our foods and drink and govern elimination of what we do not need. This is also the chakra of creativity and creation, trust and faith, and that sort of gut-knowing that intuitively signals to us when something feels right and when it doesn't. Suppression of creative expression or a dishonouring of that gut-knowing devalues and disempowers the second chakra. Artists, musicians, and healers often have strong second chakras.

The third chakra, known as the solar plexus chakra, is the ego or power chakra. Governing the area between the navel and the rib cage, it incorporates the liver, gall bladder, spleen, stomach, pancreas, kidneys and adrenals—more organs than any other chakra. Logical rather than artistic, cunning, suspicious, and very responsible, the third chakra encapsulates all those concepts about self: Who am I? Who am I supposed to be? What should I be? This is the chakra that exerts and responds to authority and power, expectations, self-control, and self-acceptance. The third chakra is usually depicted as yellow.

The fourth chakra is the heart chakra, usually depicted as green, and it governs not only the heart but also the thymus and lungs. The heart chakra connects us with others through love and emotional understanding, and allows us to really "see" and "feel" and "appreciate" other people and the world around us. As the central chakra of the seven, a strong heart chakra holds us in balance. Most traditional cultures believed that the heart was the core of the body, responsible for thought as well as emotion. Modern scientists are now just recognizing that the heart, like the brain, has its own nervous system and decision-making neurons, and that it is the electrical waves from the heart that pull the brain and other organs into synchonicity, not the other way around[134].

The fifth, or throat, chakra, usually depicted on colour charts as turquoise or light blue, is all about expression. This chakra governs the thyroid and parathyroid glands as well as the mouth, teeth, and throat area. Eden describes the chakra energy in the throat as energy chambers that extend up and down the throat with energy moving upwards in some chambers and downward in others. Some of the chambers build up and synthesize energy with others break energy down. Eden suggests that when the throat chakra is out of balance, people have trouble either speaking up (putting ideas together and expressing them) or shutting up (receiving and absorbing ideas). Sore throats, chronic colds, earaches, and problems with the thyroid or parathyroid glands are often indicative of throat chakra imbalances.

The sixth chakra, sometimes called the third-eye chakra, is located in the middle of the forehead just above the eyebrows and is usually depicted as indigo, a deep, rich blue. The sixth chakra is most often associated with psychic development, ranging from that vague sort of sixth sense or subtle knowing that most folks experience to full-blown clairvoyance, clairaudience, and self-transcendence. Within our intellect-bound Western culture, however, the sixth chakra is most often "crowded and dense with thought" according to Eden, and most of us consider that "normal". People who hear voices that others don't hear, or see things that others don't see— especially if they are not seeking this experience—are often labelled as psychotic and prescribed psychiatric medication to curb the experience.

In the chakra system, the seventh chakra, at the crown of the head, is believed to be our link with cosmic consciousness and a mystical sense of oneness with the universe. Seventh chakra organs are the brain, pituitary gland, and pineal gland. Usually associated with violet or ultra-violet/white light, the seventh chakra can be developed through meditation or prayer. When a strong opening of the seventh chakra occurs spontaneously, however, it can be an overwhelming experience, and those who have a well-developed seventh chakra without corresponding development of other chakras are likely to be perceived as "spacey," out of touch with reality, or operating in a different world. As with a strong sixth chakra, individuals with strong, uncontrolled development in the seventh chakra often find themselves resorting to psychiatric prescriptions to enable "normal" function in the modern Western world.

There is a tendency among new-Agers to emphasize development of the sixth and seventh chakras, but in reality, keeping a balance within each chakra and between all of the chakras is essential for good mind and body health. Over-emphasizing one chakra over another can create or exasperate an imbalance. No one chakra is better or more important than another—that would be like saying your liver is more important than your spleen, or your kidneys are more important than your brain, or your extensor muscles are more important than your flexor muscles. That said, some energy practitioners encourage an emphasis on the lower chakras, or lower *dan tien* if following the Chinese qi system, as this is believed to be the primary energy storage and grounding area for the body.

Three brains

There is an interesting physical corollary to the concept of bodily energy centres, particularly the head/heart/hara version that comes from China and Japan. Although most Western scientists and physicians do not openly accept the difficult-to-measure existence and effect of body energy centres, they have observed the importance of the heart and gut regions in running our bodies, and often in influencing our minds.

Most of us know we have neurons—"brain cells" we often call them, but they are actually electrically excitable nerve cells—in our brains and spinal cords, but are less likely to know that our hearts and digestive tracts also have neurons and localized nervous system centres just like the "main" head brain does. These secondary brains, like the brain inside the skull, are capable of perceiving stimuli, responding to it, and adapting responses to stimuli as a situation changes.[135]

Neurons transmit information between each other through the electrical and chemical signalling of neurotransmitters, including serotonin, dopamine, adrenalin (epinephrine), and acetylcholine. You might remember from Chapter 4 how altering the brain's neurochemical production and flow was a key concept in the development of several types of psychiatric drugs. What wasn't understood at that time was the role these neurotransmitters play in transmitting information between neurons elsewhere in the body.

To get an idea of the importance of the heart brain, for example, consider this: the electric field generated by the heart is about a hundred times more powerful than that generated by the brain, and the heart's magnetic field is about five thousand times stronger than the brain's magnetic field.[136] Active neurotransmitters in the heart include the well known epinephrine (adrenalin, the fight/flight hormone that increases the heart rate and dilates blood vessels), norepinephrine (raises blood pressure), acetylcholine (slows the heartbeat and lowers blood pressure)[137], and oxytocin (the mothering, feel-good-after-sex, and bonding hormone).

The digestive tract brain, also known as the enteric nervous system, contains as many neurons as the spinal cord.[138] Neurotransmitters released by the gut include acetylcholine and noradrenalin (norepinephrine), and the digestive tract also contains about eighty percent of the body's serotonin (the feel-good neurotransmitter and hormone) manufactured from food in the intestines.

Although the "head brain" is responsible for rational thought and decision-making, the heart and gut brain centres react and respond so quickly and automatically to emotion-generating situations, as well as to memories that have a strong emotional component, that they can short-circuit the thinking part of the brain with ease.

Fields

If the concepts of energy lines and chakra centres is a little too "new-agey" for more science-minded folk, there are equally challenging concepts emerging from the realm of quantum physics, a branch of science that emerged in the 1900s starting with Einstein's observation on the relationship between mass and energy (the old $E=MC^2$).

Quantum physics looks at what happens with matter and energy at the sub-atomic level, with particle/energy packets/waves smaller than an atom. The rules of Newtonian physics that seem to govern our grosser world break down in a place where something is either a particle or wave or energy packet depending entirely upon what the observer wants to measure. Furthermore, these particle/wave/energy packets seem to communicate with each other instantaneously over vast distances, as if time and distance are of no consequence at all.

These observations of sub-atomic particle/e-packets have lead quantum theorists to postulate a "field," or several fields (quantum, electro-magnetic, gravitational, zero-point) that hold us all together in an invisible and dynamic web of energy and information exchange that is in a constant state of flux.

Traditional biologists tend to ignore any evidence of these phenomena in complex biological systems, and medical professionals are even more reluctant to rock the Newtonian boat. There are some exceptions.

The concept of a morphic field is the child of British biologist Rupert Sheldrake who spent many years observing how schools of fish, swarms of bees, and murmurations of starlings could be made up of individual entities yet move in large groups as a single unit with a precision that could not be accounted for by assuming they look at their neighbours and mentally process what they need to do next in the group move. Sheldrake proposed that individuals (animal and human), like quantum particles, can "entangle" and subliminally affect others that are a part of their "tangle".

Furthermore, entanglement can extend over time and through space, so that rats (for example) that learn to run a maze seem to pass on the ability to run that maze to their progeny (or to learn the running of it much more quickly than their parents) and, more astonishingly, that rats unrelated to and at a totally different location from these original maze rats, when presented with the same maze, master it more quickly than did the original rats. The learned information, it would seem, has been made accessible to other rats through both time and space.[139]

Another far-reaching concept from the biological quantum fold came from researchers' attempts in the early 1900s to discover just where, exactly, memories are stored in the brain. (Anti-vivisectionists look away now!) Animals were trained with food rewards and/or electric shocks to perform various activities, and then different parts of their brains were damaged to determine which part had to be damaged to destroy their memory of the maze or sequence or pattern or activity they had learned.

Researchers were astonished to discover that there was no particular part of the brain that appeared to store the animals' memories. Even animals whose brains had been virtually destroyed through cutting or burning or removal of large brain portions could still "remember" how to perform the tasks[140].

The studies led neuroscientist Carl Pribram, working in collaboration with physicist David Bohm, to speculate that perhaps the brain stores information holographically. Since each part of a hologram contains the whole hologram, and since holograms can contain vast amounts of information in almost infinitesimally small spaces, the concept seems to fit the observation that memories can be retained regardless of the part of a brain that is damaged.

If every neuron in the brain contains memory preserved holographically, rather than each memory being stored as an individual item in a specific brain location, then memories are likely to be distributed throughout the neuronal network (which may include heart and gut neurons, if you want to extend this idea to include the more recent observations that these areas are also neuronal centres).

Holograms are created from wave interference patterns, which suggests that memories are—at the sub-atomic level—created from that quantum "stuff" of energy expressed as waves. What we think of as "perception" and "memory" and "thinking" and "visualization" are all apparently taking place in a quantum physics way with energy, waves, and interference patterns.

A few scientists and system theorists have taken this a step further and suggested that memory isn't contained in the brain at all, but rather in "the field" (like Sheldrake's morphic field, or systems theorist Ervin László's Akashic field[141]), and that rather than being the memory storage device we've so long assumed, the brain functions instead as a transmitter and receiver tuned into the field.

A very practical, technological application of this concept can be seen with the relationship between a computer (brain) and the internet (field). The parallel is pretty apt. According to this idea, your brain only pulls into awareness and stores that to which it pays attention and that which is of personal relevance. There is an infinitely vast and constantly growing cloud of information available that the brain does not bother with because it does not recognize it is there, or because the information is not recognized as of personal relevance. On the other hand, stuff you have personally stored "in the cloud" is generally retrieved with ease.

Before going on to one way this idea has been explored in the therapeutic health arena, I'd just like to once again raise the possibility that if this model is valid, what we call schizophrenia may involve some sort of uncontrolled tapping in to aspects of "the field" that most people can more effectively filter out.

EFT & matrix reimprinting

The Emotional Freedom Technique (EFT) process, also known as tapping, was developed by Gary Craig in the 1990s,[142] based an earlier process called Thought Field Therapy (TFT) developed by Roger Callahan in the 1980s.

In his book *The EFT Manual*, Craig explains how strong negative emotions and/or the disruption of the body's energy flow along the meridians are fundamental causes of much dis-ease, both mental and physical. The process of tapping on specific acupuncture energy points coupled with focussed awareness of body responses and symptoms and combined with vocalization of self-love affirmations creates a powerful yet easy-to-use and non-invasive tool for resolving a whole variety of issues.

It may look and sound a little weird, but EFT is surprisingly effective for such a simple tool, and anyone can learn how to do it and benefit from the results. While some people have experienced seemingly miraculous cures for a whole cornucopia of physical and mental problems over very little time, EFT is less likely to create powerful break-throughs as a self-administered self-help technique. Even so, something that enables you to regulate your anxiety level from, say, 8/10 down to 3/10, or a similar result with overcoming arthritic pain or whatever else is distressing you, within a few minutes, has got to be a seriously valuable technique to learn.

You can find numerous good (and some not-so-good) youtube videos demonstrating how to do EFT for many minor issues, some inviting you to tap along with the presenter and experience results for yourself. While amateur self-therapy is great for the small stuff, it is important to work with a trained EFT therapist for really big issues.

The same is also true for matrix reimprinting, a powerful way of addressing big issues that incorporates EFT as part of the process.

Whether memories and other mind stuff are actually held within a field or web or matrix outside the brain as some quantum thinkers believe, or whether this is just a useful metaphor, the concept presents a valuable key for clearing troublesome emotions of past trauma and creating life changes.

Karl Dawson developed the matrix reimprinting process while doing some EFT work with his clients[143].

Dawson assumed the concept of a field (he called it a matrix) as the depository for memories, which he called Energetic Consciousness Holograms or ECHOs. According to Dawson, ECHOs of trauma are created by a state of emotional overwhelm whereby the unconscious (or subconscious) mind stores the memory/event in the matrix so that the conscious mind can get on with life. However, the ECHO resurfaces whenever a similar situation arises, and on a cellular level, the body responds to each new event—or even simple conscious recall of an old event that was troublesome—as if it were a real-life-now danger.

In the process of matrix reimprinting, the earliest conscious memory of a triggering incident is recalled, and the person at the time the ECHO was created (in some psychological circles they call this person-you-used-to-be the "inner child" or a "soul fragment") is treated as the client. Using EFT, the older self mentally taps on the ECHO self while physically tapping on themselves (or, in a therapeutic setting, the therapist will tap on the client).

Because this is "reimprinting", while this process is going on, the older self is encouraged to allow the younger self ECHO to share how s/he is feeling and to bring in any other resources that might be helpful for resolving and dissipating the trauma. Other resources might include the wisdom and awareness of the older and wiser self, mentors, friends, family, angels, Jesus, healing light, a magical talisman, whatever. The process trusts that the older self and the ECHO will know who or what will be helpful in the situation. At the end of the process, the ECHO may choose to stay in that place with more resilience and a more positive outcome, or may choose to go elsewhere, or may want to reunite with the current Self.

It will be clear from this very brief explanation of matrix reimprinting that a lot of what occurs goes on inside the head of the once-traumatized person, usually guided by someone with experience using matrix reimprinting. In the process, the traumatic memory may or may not be changed but the emotional charge it carries and its impact on similar or triggered future events will be dissipated.

This process is similar in concept to the time line processes mentioned earlier, although that is a simpler process that does not incorporate tapping, and Brandon Bays' more convoluted but powerful journey work[144].

Control dramas

Another way of looking at the relationship between emotion, energy, and how a person responds in a particular situation, particularly within a relationship, involves understanding the role of control. In his book *The Celestine Prophecy*, author James Redfield introduces the idea of the control drama. His model assumes that we are not only creatures of energy, but that we seek to enhance our own energy when in relationship with others. The control drama clarifies how many of us may do this.

I found this another useful way to recognize and understand why people behave the way they do, just as personality subtypes and characteristics like introvert/extrovert and matcher/mismatcher allow us to understand better how we participate in the world and how those around us do so.

In both the original book and in the companion volume *The Celestine Prophecy: An Experiential Guide*, Redfield identifies four ways that people take energy from others, or protect themselves from others perceived as energy vampires. The desired energy may be perceived as love, recognition, respect, attention, approval, admiration, and/or support. A positive flow of this kind of energy enhances any relationship. However, when one party seeks to take unoffered energy from another, there are a number of strategies that are commonly used.

The strongest and most active way to pull energy from others is through intimidation. The intimidator forces people to pay attention to him/her through loudness, strength, threat, intimidation, anger, and emotional outbursts. By making others feel small, threatened or inadequate, s/he gains strength. His/her inner struggle is, ironically, a fear of being controlled or of not having enough. The intimidator may justify his/her behaviour with claims like "If I don't do this, no one else will," or "If I don't get there first, someone else will," or "No one takes care of me so I have to do it myself, " or "Nobody tells me what to do."

The interrogator, on the other hand, is less brash and uses questions and criticism to create influence and control others. S/he keeps a close watch over others, questioning their motives and responses, and is constantly comparing the actions of others to how s/he would do things. In doing so, s/he is able to feel superior and more powerful than others, or at the least better able to gain their attention. The interrogator's inner struggle is a fear of being alone, unwanted, unvalued, or unheard, and this is reflected in a string of inquiries: Where are you going? Why are you doing that? Why didn't you...? Why would you do that? A question demands a response, attention, and recognition of the asker.

The aloof individual holds power by remaining passive and not responding to others. This person may come across as disinterested, unavailable, contrary, or even sneaky because s/he tends to be caught up in his/her own internal world, but this is often a protective mechanism activated most often by interrogators, but sometimes by intimidators or victims. The aloof person's inner struggle is with a fear of inadequacy, an inability to trust his or her own judgement and feelings, or a fear of entrapment.

The victim—Redfield calls the victim the "Poor me"—pulls sympathy (and thus energy) from others through being needy, whinging and whining, or virtuous martyrdom: "Don't worry, I'll be fine." Their inner struggle is with the fear they won't be noticed, recognized, cared for, or needed, and they most often seek attention from intimidators who are often subconsciously perceived as strong and powerful protectors.

Relationships are always a sort of dance. Thus victims often dance with intimidators, for example trying to make them feel guilty—"Look how you're making me cry"—to stop an attack and re-establish a positive flow of energy. Interrogators, on the other hand, often dance with the aloof, trying to pull attention through a barrage of questions, which the aloof person may deflect by not responding at all, or through clipped or inappropriate answers.

Of course all of these role/traits can be reframed as positive strengths: the intimidator can also be a strong leader, assertive and confident. The interrogator can be a strong advocate or teacher. The aloof person is often an independent and creative thinker capable of scientific breakthroughs, artistic achievements, or profound spiritual growth. And those who have experienced victimhood can be compassionate reformers, social workers and healers.

Redfield's advice to those caught up in control dramas—which, by the way, he believes usually develop as childhood behaviours learned in response to parental control dramas—is to become aware of your own control dramas and the control dramas played out by the people you interact with. How do you respond to them? What inner struggle issue or insecurities lurk underneath your own behaviour or the behaviour of others? If you can identify the drama occurring, you are able to notice the power or energy struggle being played out. Becoming aware of what is happening is a valuable first step in making positive choices about continuing or changing the drama. (I used to teach high school English, and I'd describe this as looking at the *structure* of a story or film rather than the plot. They're not the same thing.)

Remember that unlike personality profile characteristics, control dramas are dynamic and constantly changing, and they always involve more than one person. Your role in one control drama may be quite different from your role in another control drama. You might play victim with your partner, be aloof with your mother, and become an interrogator with your children. Or you might play intimidator one day, and victim the next.

Understanding how the control dramas are being played out allows you to get down to the fabric that underlies a relationship. If that relationship needs work, awareness of the needs and methods of the participants is a first step towards adjustment and repair.

Recommended books

Lynne McTaggart's *The Field: The Quest for the Secret Force of the Universe* explores the significance of the quantum universe as regards health, psychology, and relationships. If body, mind, consciousness, and the zero-point field ring bells for you, and you enjoy exploring the serendipitous connections that aid scientific and philosophical developments with a quantum beat, you should find this book worthwhile.

Energy Medicine by Donna Eden, mentioned earlier in this chapter, is outstanding. Packed with information about the body's energy systems, how to read them, and how to optimize your health by working with them, this superb book is both insightful and practical.

I also really like Kenneth S. Cohen's book *The Way of Qigong: The Art and Science of Chinese Energy Healing*. Cohen shares the history of qi gong and the science that supports the practice; suggests a variety of meditations, breathing practices, and movements that you CAN learn from a book; offers dietary and other health advice; and gives guidance to enable the reader to grow and move with grace, power, and awareness.

Certainly thought-provoking is Bruce Lipton's *The Biology of Belief*. Lipton, a cell biologist, discovered that cells respond intelligently to stimuli regardless of whether or not they have a nucleus, leading him to posit that it's not DNA that determines the choices cells (and larger organisms) make, but their perception of their environment. In the book, Lipton challenges several conventional assumptions about the roles of belief and energy in creating health and well-being—a master re-framer!

An experienced physician, obstetrician and gynaecologist, Lissa Rankin published *Mind Over Medicine: Scientific Proof That You Can Heal Yourself* in 2013 following her observation that patients often resolved all manner of resistant and chronic conditions when they were invited to explore such basic (but rarely asked by doctors) questions as "What does your body need in order to heal?" and "If your [dis-ease] could talk to you, what would it say?" Rather than dismiss these results as a placebo effect, Rankin believes we should celebrate the news that in up to 80% of cases, the mind is capable of healing the body without pharmaceutical or surgical intervention. Although not specifically about the role of energy and emotion in creating mental and physical illness/health, this book examines health and illness—both physical and mental—in a holistic way that is enlightening and empowering, and reflects a growing paradigm shift in our understanding of dis-ease.

British biologist Rupert Sheldrake has written several books that challenge a number of conventional scientific beliefs. His most recent, titled *The Science Delusion* in the UK and *Science Set Free* in the US, examines questions like "is matter unconscious?" and "are minds confined to brains?" His seminal book, *Morphic Resonance*, was first published in 1981. You can also find interesting talks and interviews with Sheldrake on the internet.

Karl Dawson's book *Matrix Reimprinting Using EFT: Rewrite Your Past, Transform Your Future* covers the EFT process and matrix reimprinting. It is an easy-to-read, insightful and practical guide to understanding and using these powerful processes.

Shakuntala Modi's book *Remarkable Healings: A Psychiatrist Discovers Unexpected Roots of Mental and Physical Illness* was mentioned briefly in the previous chapter. In addition to crediting the power of past life events and soul fragmentation as significant causes of mental illness, she also argues a case for spirit possession by a variety of entities, echoing the work of Joseph Gassner (see Chapter 3). This is a line of inquiry I have not pursued in this book, but the interested reader may find Modi's book worth seeking out.

Chapter 9: Transcendence

Often the journey to mental health is, deep down, a search for self, a quest to discover who you really are, how you work, and what your purpose in life might be. It may not seem that way at the time, of course, but often it is. In this final chapter, I'd like to look at the road to enlightenment (one of many!) that may have begun with some form of mental distress or dis-ease.

The Indian mystic Osho wrote

> I'm simply saying that there is a way to be sane. I'm saying that you can get rid of all this insanity created by the past in you. Just by being a simple witness of your thought processes.
>
> It's simply sitting silently, witnessing the thoughts, passing before you. Just witnessing, not interfering, not even judging, because the moment you judge you have lost the pure witness. The moment you say "this is good, this is bad," you have already jumped onto the thought process.
>
> It takes a little time to create a gap between the witness and the mind. Once the gap is there, you are in for a great surprise, that you are not the mind, that you are the witness, a watcher.
>
> And this process of watching is the very alchemy of real religion. Because as you become more and more deeply

rooted in witnessing, thoughts start disappearing. You are, but the mind is utterly empty.

That's the moment of enlightenment. That is the moment that you become for the first time an unconditioned, sane, really free human being.

"That's all right for Osho," you might be thinking. "He was a mystic. Me? I don't have time to spend hours sitting cross-legged on the floor in deep meditation waiting for some profound *witness* revelation! Geez!"

But it's not as hard as it sounds.

Finding the witness

In his book *The Mandala of Being: Discovering the Power of Awareness*, Richard Moss offers a really marvellous exercise. Try this as you are reading it (and really do TRY it, don't just read about it):

First, even as you are reading this, become aware of your breathing. Don't change anything, just follow the movement of the air as it is pulled in through your nose or mouth, and become aware of how it fills your lungs, how your breathing may pause briefly right before you switch between exhale and inhale, how the air moves in and out of your body. Notice how your chest rises and falls to accommodate the air in your lungs. Now notice how, before I called attention to your breathing, you weren't even aware of it.

Consider, then, what "attention" means. What shifted or changed within you so you could become aware of your breathing? How, exactly, does attention change? Who or what changes that attention?

Let's examine this question a bit more. Imagine that your breathing is like a kite flying in the sky above you, and notice that you didn't notice the kite until it was pointed out to you. Now imagine that your attention is the string that connects you to the breathing kite.

Turn your attention around away from the breathing and go back down the kite's string to...who or what is holding the string of attention? Who or what is flying the kite?

It's easy to say, "Me, I'm flying the kite," but many people perceive "nothing" or "emptiness" or "space." If you are thinking "me", then visualise where, exactly, the string is coming from. Is it coming from your head (forehead? Crown?)? Your chest? Your gut? This is the string of attention, remember. Where does the attention come from?

If this string of attention comes from some part of your body, try visualising that you [yourself, your body] are a kite. Now imagining yourself as the kite, follow the string back down to who or what is paying attention to this image of you.

If you come up with another image, follow the string on that one, as many times as you need to. Eventually you will reach the point where the inevitable answer is "nothing" or "I don't know" or "emptiness". This is the witness. Rest on that thought for a moment, then...

Remember what you had for breakfast, or a meal you had yesterday. As soon as you endeavour to recall this information, it will be available there for you. Imagine, now, that this memory of your meal is a kite, and the string, again, is your attention on that memory. Follow the string to see who or what is holding this memory. Where does your attention to this memory begin? Is it in the present or the past?

Now think about something you will do tomorrow. Notice how as you do this, a "kite" appears that contains information about this future event that hasn't even happened yet. Examine this future event. What details do you notice? Then, as before, reverse your attention down the string to you, the attention holder. Who or what is creating this attention? Who or what is creating the kite? Where is this event? Is it in the future? In the present? In the past? Who is the "me" that holds the string? And who, now, is the witness who is observing "me" holding the string of attention on the kite of breath, of yesterday, of tomorrow?

The value of now

In his book *The Mandala of Being*, and in his subsequent book *Inside-Out Healing,* Moss observes that whenever our thoughts are not resting in the present moment of now, they are caught up re-creating some past event, creating a future event, focussing on "me", or focussing on another person (you) or thing (it). Those are the only four directions, according to Moss, that our attention can go when it leaves the witness-moment.

Why is this important? When you are caught up in the story that you are creating about why you feel a particular way—and Moss reminds us that we are self-creating stories here—you are allowing all kinds of beliefs, assumptions, experiences and worries to colour your perception.

"Me" stories we create about ourselves are often things like "I deserve (or don't deserve) this," "I am (or am not) capable of doing this," or "I should (or should not) do or think this." Mostly, these stories allow us to glorify ourselves, or make ourselves special, or criticize ourselves through judgements.

"You" and "it" stories allow us to judge others (or things or situations) by our personal standards, usually by comparing how things are with how we believe they should be, and allow us to shift the blame for things we don't like away from ourselves and on to others. "You" stories might include themes like, "S/he just makes me so angry!" and "S/he shouldn't do that." These stories also include things we believe about money, about the world, about our environment—all that stuff "out there".

Past stories allow us to feel pride and regret, joy and sadness, and to justify how we feel in the present. "Past" stories might include "If I hadn't done that, I wouldn't be in this mess now," or "I could never live up to my father's expectations either."

Future stories can make us feel eager and hopeful, or worried and anxious. "What if I try that and it doesn't work out?" or "Once I've done this, I'll be able to do that!" Yet none of these story spaces operates in isolation.

Let's take an example. In the space of "now" you may wish to explore some emotion that is a problem for you, let's say "anger," which you can physically feel in the "now" with a sort of churn in your gut area, your breathing quicker than normal, perhaps a tightness in your chest or throat.

And when you move from "now" (sensations) and think "I am angry" (the "me" point of view) you might be thinking something like "I don't deserve this." And that may lead to a "you" story and thinking something like, "S/he doesn't treat me right. It's not my fault that I'm feeling like this. S/he causes this!"

And that may lead you to a past story, something like "I've been through this before, so many times! I'm sick and tired of it! Why do I always end up surrounded by people who make me feel like dirt?"

And that can lead to a future projection, something like "I don't see any way out of this. I'm just always stuck dealing with self-righteous people who don't get where I'm coming from, and never will. And even if I change this or that in my life, I'd just be trying to adapt myself to what they want me to be, and I don't see that making it any better."

Yet, when you step back into "now," there is a sense of spaciousness, neutrality, and awareness without judgement that is remarkably freeing. We can't spend our lives in the witness/now box, of course, but it is a useful reminder that from that vantage point, there is no judgement, no assumption, no belief barging in to malform our life experience. When in the "now", Moss encourages the use of affirmations like "I am sufficient as I am."

It is also a useful reminder that when we jump into the me, you, past, or future positions, we are creating stories that we then assume are reality rather than simply our maps of reality. Moss does not advise attempting to change our stories, or create more positive ones, but simply to recognize stories for what they are. In a way, this Moss mandala work like an extension of the Heart Math freeze frame process mentioned in chapter 7.

There is a huge amount of wisdom revealed in Moss's work, and I've only briefly touched on it here. To really appreciate the witness/now approach to dealing with the hurly burly of life with understanding and grace, I recommend reading his books, doing a retreat that explores this process, or consulting a practitioner familiar with using Moss's mandala work.

Parts integration

Sometimes our beliefs and stories create conflicts that snag us up when we are trying to move forward in life. There's a simple NLP process that I like very much that addresses this problem. It's called parts integration, and its useful whenever you feel like one part of you wants one thing and another part of you wants something else.

For example you might, on one hand, want to get out more and spend more time with other people, yet on the other hand, you don't feel comfortable doing that. In fact, you may feel a sense of stress or discomfort whenever confronted with making a decision that triggers that particular parts conflict.

In the parts integration process, you explore each part by giving it (or recognizing it has) some physical characteristics, and then ask each part what it wants for you in doing what it does. A series of questions usually reveals that both parts actually want the same thing for you, but they each go about achieving that goal in different ways. The ultimate desire of each part usually turns out to be some profound human need or desire like safety or freedom or joy or love or happiness. Once it is understood that the parts have the same positive desire for you, they can be integrated back into the self, and knowing that in future, they will work together towards that goal rather than in opposition.

Maybe it sounds pretty flaky when described this way, but the power of the process can be profound. In a sense, the integration of parts allows us to transcend internal conflicts in such a way that one becomes aware of more important aspects of life that we too often forget in the day-to-day hurly burly of existence.

Whether you believe there are two (or more) actual "parts" of you, or whether this is a more metaphorical process doesn't matter. The unconscious mind accepts this process as real and significant.

Other healing processes which use a similar concept include matrix reimprinting and the shamanic practice of soul retrieval. Regardless of how strange, unrealistic, and downright bizarre this sort of processing of parts and subsequent integration might seem in a scientific light, it is capable of being truly transformational in terms of healing power.

Alchemy

In the Middle Ages, alchemists—the ancestors, if you will, of modern chemists—sought the elusive secret of transmutation of base (meaning easily corroded or damaged, and thus not particularly valuable) metals such as iron and lead into gold, and attempted to create life elixirs and magical tonics to enhance youthfulness and longevity. Although they did not succeed in these goals, they did enhance our world with new methods of testing and working with ores; new dyes, paints, cosmetics, and various extracts; and they developed the process of distillation.

Modern chemists have been more successful in manifesting gold from not-gold, although not through any way the early alchemists envisaged. Through chemical pharmacy, base mentals (no typo here, but perhaps a bad pun) have been used as a ready market for the creation of great wealth for pharmaceutical companies and their investors. The elixir of life, on the other hand, remains elusive. Or does it?

This book began with a historical perspective on the care and treatment of the mentally ill. Modern scientific and medical approaches involve a variety of physical procedures and chemical manipulations of the brain and body ostensibly to elicit a change in perception and behaviour. These processes are based wholly on the assumption that someone who is mentally ill has some physical aspect of their brain that is broken and needs to be fixed. And significantly, by someone else.

Yet the real alchemy that is possible for those deemed "mentally ill"—and indeed, for all of us—is not something that comes from a bottle of potion or a blister pack of pills conjured up in some chemical laboratory, but the personal transformation that occurs with increased self-understanding and awareness, introspection, gratitude, acceptance, and forgiveness, including (and this is really important) forgiveness of, and love for, self and parts of self.

Real alchemy means making changes to the map of the world we carry with us and reframing the events in our lives to enable and empower ourselves to be the best we can be regardless of the circumstances that appear to shape our lives.

The EFT process begins with a tapping on the outside edge of the hand and the words, "Even though I have this [anxiety, headache, sore knee... whatever the problem is], I deeply and completely love and accept myself." Here, I think, cloaked in a process that some might find vaguely inane, is one of the most powerful paths to mental wholeness and wellness we have: "I love and accept myself."

As we grow to know who and what we really are—who is the witness, and why are we witnessing this?—and as we ask the questions and seek the answers within ourselves, we may come to an awareness of peace and well-being that far supersedes anything that comes out of a bottle. In truth, the alchemist, and the elixir of life itself, exists within us all.

Notes
ᘯᕉᕉᘳ

[1] Statistics provided by Medco Health Solutions as reported in Wang, S. S. (2011, November 16). Psychiatric Drug Use Spreads. *The Wall Street Journal*, Asia Edition. Retrieved from http://online.wsj.com/article/SB10001424052970203503 204577040431792673066.html See also Smith, B. L. (2012). Inappropriate Prescribing. *Monitor on Psychology*, 43, 6, retrieved December 2013 from http://www.apa.org/monitor/2012/06/prescribing.aspx

[2] http://money.cnn.com/magazines/fortune/fortune500/2 009/performers/industries/profits/ It is an interesting list.

[3] Bartholow, M. (2012, July 10). Top 200 Drugs of 2011. *Pharmacy Times*. Retrieved from http://www.pharmacytimes.com/publications/issue/2012 /July2012/Top-200-Drugs-of-2011

[4] The word purgatory is related to purge and both derive from the Latin verb purgare, to purify.

[5] *A foreign view of England in the reigns of George I and George II: The letters of Monsieur Cesar de Saussure to his family*, translated and edited by Madame Van Muyden, retrieved from http://archive.org/details/foreignviewofeng00sausuoft

[6] Richards, R.J. (1998). Rhapsodies on a Cat-Piano, or Johann Christian Reil and the Foundations of Romantic Psychiatry. Retrieved from http://home.uchicago.edu/~rjr6/articles/Rhapsodies%20 on%20a%20Cat-Piano.pdf

[7] Whitaker, R. (2001). *Mad in America: Bad Science, Bad Medicine, and the Enduring Mistreatment of the Mentally Ill*. New York: Basic Books.

[8] Ibid. Much of the historical material in this chapter is explored in greater detail in this excellent book.

[9] http://hpy.sagepub.com/content/21/4/471.full.pdf

[10] http://www.pbs.org/wgbh/amex/nash/filmmore/ps_ict.html

[11] Healy, D. (2011). *Mania: A Short History of Bipolar Disorder*. Baltimore: John Hopkins University Press.

[12] Cade, J.F. (1949) Lithium salts in the treatment of psychotic excitement. Reprinted in *Bull World Health Organisation*, 2000; 78(4):518-520. Retrieved from http://www.ncbi.nlm.nih.gov/pmc/articles/PMC2560740/

[13] http://www.ncbi.nlm.nih.gov/pmc/articles/PMC2560740/pdf/10885180.pdf

[14] Healy, D. (2011). *Mania: A Short History of Bipolar Disorder*. Baltimore: John Hopkins University Press.

[15] Lader, M. (1991). History of benzodiazepine dependence. *Journal of Substance Abuse Treatment*, 8(102), 53-59.

[16] http://www.bonkersinstitute.org/medshow/benzedrinearmy.html

[17] http://www.ncbi.nlm.nih.gov/pmc/articles/PMC2377281/

[18] Ibid.

[19] From Ellenberg, H.F. (1970). The Discovery of the Unconscious: The History and Evolution of Dynamic Psychiatry, Chapter 2. Retrieved from http://www.mhweb.org/mpc_course/ellenberger.pdf

[20] Ban, T. (2007) Fifty years chlorpromazine: a historical perspective. *Neuropsychiatric Disease and Treatment*, 3(4): 495-500. Retrieved April 2013 from http://www.ncbi.nlm.nih.gov/pmc/articles/PMC2655089/#!po=20.8333

[21] Whitaker, R. (2001). *Mad in America: Bad Science, Bad Medicine, and the Enduring Mistreatment of the Mentally Ill*. New York: Basic Books.

[22] Ibid.

[23] Ibid.

[24] Ibid.

[25] Ibid.

[26] Healy, D. (2004). *Let Them Eat Prozac*. New York and London: New York University Press.

[27] Photos of early advertisements are available on line. Just go to Google Images and search for the drug you are looking for

[28] Healy, D. (2004). *Let Them Eat Prozac*. New York and London: New York University Press.

[29] Photos of early advertisements are available on line. Just go to Google Images and search for the drug you are looking for.

[30] Dokoupil, T. (2009). How mother found her helper. *Newsweek*, retrieved from http://www.thedailybeast.com/newsweek/2009/01/21/how-mother-found-her-helper.html

[31] Metzl, J. (2003). "Mother's Little Helper": The crisis of psychoanalysis and the Miltown Resolution. Gender & History, 15(2), 240-267, retrieved from http://www.med.umich.edu/psych/faculty/metzl/07_Metzl.pdf

[32] Sandler, M. (1990). Monoamine oxidase inhibitors in depression: History and mythology. *Journal of Psychopharmacology*, 4(3), 136-139.

[33] Ibid. "Effective," of course, is a fairly loose term.

[34] Whitaker, R. (2010). *Anatomy of an Epidemic*. New York: Crown Publishing.

[35] Thase, M. E., Trivedi, M. H., and Rush, A.J. (1995). MAOIs in the contemporary treatment of depression. *Neuropsychopharmacology*, 12(3), 185-219.

[36] Whitaker, R. (2001). *Mad in America: Bad Science, Bad Medicine, and the Enduring Mistreatment of the Mentally Ill*. New York: Basic Books.

[37] Lader, M. (1991). History of benzodiazepine dependence. *Journal of Substance Abuse Treatment*, 8(102), 53-59.

[38] Metzl, J. (2003). "Mother's Little Helper": The crisis

of psychoanalysis and the Miltown Resolution. *Gender & History*, 15(2), 240-267, retrieved from http://www.med.umich.edu/psych/faculty/metzl/07_Metzl.pdf

39 López-Munoz, F. and Alamo, C. (2009). Monoaminergic neurotransmission: The history of the discovery of antidepressants from 1950s until today. *Current Pharmaceutical Design*, 15, 1563-1586, retrieved from http://www.biopsychiatry.com/antidepressants.pdf

40 Healy, D. (1997). *The Antidepressant Era*. Boston: Harvard University Press.

41 Schildkraut, J. J. & Katy, S. S. (1967) Biogenic amines and emotion. *Science*, 156(3771), 21-30.

42 Ashcroft, G. & Healy, D. (2000). The receptor enters psychiatry. In *The Psychopharmachologists III: Interviews by David Healy* (pp. 189-200). London: Arnold.

43 Leventhal A. M., & Antonuccio, D. O. (2009). On chemical imbalances, antidepressant, and the diagnosis of depression. *Ethical Human Psychology and Psychiatry*, 11, 199-214.

44 Wilcox, DRC, Gillan R, Hare EH. Do psychiatric patients take their drugs? *BMJ* 1965; 2: 790-2.

45 Whitaker cites numerous references for these disorders and claims. See Whitaker, R. (2001). *Mad in America: Bad science, bad medicine, and the enduring mistreatment of the mentally ill*. New York: Basic Books

46 Healy, D. (2004) *Let Them Eat Prozac*. New York and London: New York University Press.

47 Ibid., and Shorter, E. (2009) *Before Prozac: The Troubled History of Mood Disorders in Psychiatry*. Oxford: Oxford University Press.

48 Breggin, P. (2008). *Medication Madness: The Role of Psychiatric Drugs in Cases of Violence, Suicide, and Crime*. New York: St. Martin's Press.

49 Medawar, C., Hardon, A., & Herzheimer, A. (2004). Depressing research. *The Lancet*, 363(9426).

50 Healy, D. (2004) *Let Them Eat Prozac*. New York and London: New York University Press.

51 Breggin, P. (2008). *Medication Madness: The Role of Psychiatric Drugs in Cases of Violence, Suicide, and Crime.* New York: St. Martin's Press.

52 Whitaker, R. (2010). *Anatomy of an Epidemic.* New York: Crown Publishers.

53 Wong, D. T., Bymaster, F. P., and Engleman, E. A. (1995). Prozac (fluoxetine, Lilly 110141), the first selective serotonin uptake inhibitor and an antidepressant drug: Twenty years since its first publication. *Life Sciences,* 57(4), 411-441.

54 Internal Eli Lilly communication reported in Healy, D. (2004) *Let Them Eat Prozac.* New York and London: New York University Press.

55 McLean, B. (2001). A bitter pill Prozac made Eli Lilly. *Fortune,* 13 August, Retrieved from http://money.cnn.com/magazines/fortune/fortune_archiv e/2001/08/13/308077/

56 From Bashfield (1998) & Scotti & Morris (2000), retrieved from The development of the DSM http://kadi.myweb.uga.edu/The_Development_of_the_D SM.html

57 Wilson, M. (1993). DSM-III and the transformation of American psychiatry: a history. *American Journal of Psychiatry* Mar; 150(3): 399-410.

58 Much of the criticism of the DSM-V seems to be based around the DSM concept in general, that psychiatric disorders can and should be categorized like medical disorders...if you have such and such symptoms, you can (should?) be diagnosed with a particular disease which can then be treated.

59 Whitaker, R. (2010). *Anatomy of an Epidemic.* New York: Crown Publishers.

60 Strohl, M. P. (2011). Bradley's Benzedrine studies on children with behavioural disorders. *Yale Journal of Biological Medicine,* March 84(1): 27-33.

61 Whitaker, R. (2010). *Anatomy of an Epidemic.* New York: Crown Publishers.

62 Ritalin. Center for Substance Abuse Research (CESAR). University of Maryland. Retrieved from

http://www.cesar.umd.edu/cesar/drugs/ritalin.asp

[63] Willets, S. (2008). The History of Ritalin (Methylpehnidate). Retrieved from http://www.ritalinadvisor.com/history

[64] Whitaker, R. (2010). *Anatomy of an Epidemic*. New York: Crown Publishers.

[65] For some insight into how Lilly coaxed positive results out of their numerous paediatric trials for Prozac, see Whitaker, R. (2010). *Anatomy of an Epidemic*. New York: Crown Publishers

[66] Healy, D. (2012). *Pharmageddon*. Los Angeles: University of California Press.

[67] Ibid.

[68] Ibid.

[69] Evans, D. (2009, November 9). Pfizer broke the law by promoting drugs for unapproved uses. Retrieved from http://www.bloomberg.com/apps/news?pid=newsarchive&sid=a4yV1nYxCG0A

[70] Hills, J. (2013). Big pharma's big payouts. *Drugwatch*. Retrieved December 2013 from http://www.drugwatch.com/2013/12/06/big-pharma-settlements/

[71] Thrasher, S. (2010). Collateral damage: A mixed-methods study to investigate the use and withdrawal of antidepressants within a naturalistic population. Wellington, New Zealand: Victoria University master's thesis. Retrieved from http://researcharchive.vuw.ac.nz/handle/10063/1501

[72] Whitaker, R. (2010). *Anatomy of an Epidemic*. New York: Crown Publishers.

[73] Ibid.

[74] Healy, D. (2011). *Mania: A Short History of Bipolar Disorder*. Baltimore: John Hopkins University Press.

[75] Whitaker, R. (2010). *Anatomy of an Epidemic*. New York: Crown Publishers.

[76] Ibid., for a more detailed discussion of this.

[77] Healy, D. (2008). *Mania: A Short History of Bipolar Disorder*. Baltimore: John Hopkins University Press.

[78] For an insight into how this works, see Jaing, T.,

Kaufman, S., Khatri, P., & Morales, S. (2003). Pharmaceutical product introduction: Launching Eli Lilly's Serafem (A). Retrieved from https://faculty.fuqua.duke.edu/~willm/bio/TeachingMaterials/0Cases/Serafem/SarafemA_2003_wm3f.pdf

79 For one woman's account of her experience see Rebensdorf, A. (2001). Sarafem: The pimping of Prozac for PMS retrieved from http://www.alternet.org/story/11004/sarafem%3A_the_pimping_of_prozac_for_pms

80 Andreasen, N. C., Liu, D., Ziebell, S., Vora, A., & Ho, B.C. (2013). Relapse duration, treatment intensity, and brain tissue loss in schizophrenia: A prospective longitudinal study. *American Journal of Psychiatry* 2013; 170:609-615.

81 Manocha, M. and Khan, W. I. (2012). Serotonin and GI disorders: An update on clinical and experimental studies. *Clinical and Translational Gastroenterology*, 3, e13. Retrieved from http://www.nature.com/ctg/journal/v3/n4/full/ctg20128a.html

82 Vanhoutte, P. M. & Lüscher, T. F. (1986). Serotonin and the blood vessel wall. *Journal of Hypertension Supplement*, April, 4(1):S29-35. and Vanhouette, P. M. (1987). Cardiovascular effects of serotonin. *Journal of Cardiovascular Pharmacology*, 10 Supplement 3:8-11.

83 Rosen, R. C., Lane R. M. & Menza, M. (1999). Effects of SSRIs on sexual function: a critical review. *Journal of Clinical Psychopharmacology*, 19(1): 67-85.

84 Healy, D. (2012). *Pharmageddon*. Los Angeles: University of California Press.

85 Breggin, P. (2013). *Psychiatric Drug Withdrawal: A Guide for Researchers, Therapists, Patients and Their Families*. New York: Springer.

86 Ventola, C. L. (2011). Direct-to-consumer pharmaceutical advertising. *Pharmacy & Therapeutics*, October, 669-674, 681-684, retrieved from http://www.ncbi.nlm.nih.gov/pmc/articles/PMC3278148/

87 Ibid.

[88] Graber, M. A. & Weckmann, M. (2002). Pharmaceutical company internet sites as sources of information about antidepressant medications. *CNS Drugs*, 16/(6), 419-423. Retrieved from http://www.ncbi.nlm.nih.gov/pubmed/12027787

[89] Around 42% of unbranded mental health websites are funded or partially funded by pharmaceutical companies. See Read, J. & Cain, A. (2013). A literature review and meta-analysis of drug company-funded mental health websites. Acta Psychiatry Sandanavia, May 10. Retrieved from http://www.ncbi.nlm.nih.gov/pubmed/23662697

[90] Liang, B. A. & Mackey, T. (2011). Direct-to-consumer advertising with interactive internet media: Global regulation and public health issues. *JAMA*, February 23, 35(8). Retrieved from http://anesthesia.ucsd.edu/research/faculty-research/Documents/LiangMackeyJAMAeDTCA.pdf

[91] See http://www.newsinmind.com/general-news/greif-over-dsm-v-depression-criteria

[92] See Watters, E. (2010). *Crazy Like Us: The Globalization of the American Psyche*. New York: Free Press.

[93] Richard is an outstanding trainer, and the courses can be life-changing. See http://www.transformations.net.nz/

[94] Alexander, B. K. (ND). Addiction: the view from rat park. Retrieved April 2014 from http://globalizationofaddiction.ca/articles-speeches/148-addiction-the-view-from-rat-park.html

[95] Healy, D. (2012). *Pharmageddon*. Los Angeles: University of California Press.

[96] See https://www.cia.gov/library/publications/the-world-factbook/fields/2195.html

[97] Healy, D. (2012). *Pharmageddon*. Los Angeles: University of California Press.

[98] Ibid.

[99] Kirsch, I. (2010). *The Emperor's New Drugs: Exploding the Antidepressant Myth*. New York: Basic

Books.

[100]Whitaker, R. (2010). *Anatomy of an Epidemic*. New York: Crown Publishers.

[101] Salunke, B. P., Umathe, S. N., & Chavan, J. G. (2013). Effect of electromagnetic radiations on anxiety related behavior: A review. *Journal of Biomedical and Pharmaceutical Research* 2(1) 2013, 36-40, retrieved from http://jbpr.in/index.php/jbpr/article/view/85/75

[102] Ibid.

[103] See http://www.ncbi.nlm.nih.gov/books/NBK64063/ for the exact wording, and variations on different types of depression

[104] Kline, 1964, as reported in Whitaker, R. (2010). *Anatomy of an Epidemic*. New York: Crown Publishers.

[105] http://www.vivachi.co.nz/ and http://shinnickdepression.co.nz/

[106] From the BBC documentary *How to Make Better Decisions*, http://www.youtube.com/watch?v=i1OVhlRpwJc

[107] The you tube clip http://www.youtube.com/watch?v=ZknnKjTfDuo

[108] http://www.ncbi.nlm.nih.gov/books/NBK64063/

[109] See http://www.dnalc.org/view/899-DSM-IV-Criteria-for-Schizophrenia.html

[110] To find out more, visit the Hearing Voices Network at http://www.hearing-voices.org/tag/hearing-voices/, or search for a branch in your country.

[111] Waters, F. (2010). Auditory hallucinations in psychiatric illness. *Psychiatric Times*. Retrieved from http://www.psychiatrictimes.com/schizophrenia/auditory-hallucinations-psychiatric-illness

[112] Teeple, R. C., Caplan, J. P., & Stern, T. A. (2009). Visual hallucinations: Differential diagnosis and treatment. *The Primary Care Companion to the Journal of Clinical Psychiatry*, 11(1): 26-32. Retrieved from http://www.ncbi.nlm.nih.gov/pmc/articles/PMC2660156/

[113] See http://www.psychnet-uk.com/x_new_site/DSM_IV/capgras_syndrome.html

[114] Moncrieff, J., Cohen, D., & Mason, J. P. (2009). The subjective experience of taking antipsychotic medication: a content analysis of internet data. *Acta Psychiatrica Scandinavica* 2009: 1-10. Retrieved from http://www.mentalhealth.freeuk.com/acta.pdf

[115] Hall, M., Bodenhamer, B. G, Bolstad, R., & Hamblett, M. (2001). *The Structure of Personality: Modeling "Personality" Using NLP and Neuro-Semantics.* Carmarthan (UK): Crown House Publishing.

[116] From Haley, J., and Hoffman, L. (1967) *Techniques of Family Therapy.* New York: Basic Books, reprinted in Hall, M., Bodenhamer, B. G, Bolstad, R., & Hamblett, M. (2001). *The Structure of Personality: Modeling "Personality" Using NLP and Neuro-Semantics.* Carmarthan (UK): Crown House Publishing.

[117] Richard Bolstad, from Hall, M., Bodenhamer, B. G, Bolstad, R., & Hamblett, M. (2001). *The Structure of Personality: Modeling "Personality" Using NLP and Neuro-Semantics.* Carmarthan (UK): Crown House Publishing.

[118] See http://www.humanmetrics.com/cgi-win/jtypes2.asp or http://similarminds.com/jung.html The first of these asks yes/no questions, the second asks you to identify how closely you agree with the statement. When I took both, I came up with the same result, but my percentages were different. The percentages identify how closely you fit the profiles.

[119] American Psychiatric Association. (2013). *Attention Deficit/Hyperactivity Disorder.* Retrieved January 2014 from http://www.dsm5.org/Documents/ADHD%20Fact%20Sheet.pdf

[120] The following are summarized from DSM-IV (Text Revision) Definition Attention/Deficit/Hyperactivity Disorder retrieved January 2014 from https://www.msu.edu/course/cep/888/ADHD%20files/DSM-IV.htm

[121] See ADHD update: new data on the risks of medication (2006). *Harvard Medical School Family*

Health Guide retrieved January 2014 from
http://www.health.harvard.edu/fhg/updates/ADHD-update-New-data-on-the-risks-of-medication.shtml and
Collingwood, J. (2010). Side effects of ADHD medication.
Psych Central, retrieved January 2014 from
http://psychcentral.com/lib/side-effects-of-adhd-medications/0003782 and Breggin, P. (2000). Confirming
the hazards of stimulant drug treatment. *Ethical Human Sciences and Services*, 2, 3. Retrieved January 2014 from
http://breggin.com/index2.php?option=com_docman&task=doc_view&gid=29&Itemid=37

[122] Witts, B. (2009). Seeing the indigo child. *Skeptical Inquirer*. Retrieved January 2014 from
http://www.csicop.org/si/show/seeing_the_indigo_children/

[123] A deliberate double misquote. The original, "Lay on, Macduff, and damned be him who first cries "Hold! Enough!" (from Shakespeare's *MacBeth*) is often misquoted as "Lead on Macduff."

[124] See http://www.heartmath.org/ and I also recommend the book *The Heart Math Solution*, by founder Doc Childre, ©2000 (although the digital edition is © 2011).

[125] Rein, G., Atkinson, M., & McCraty, R. (1995). The physiological and psychological effects of compassion and anger." *Journal of Advancement in Medicine*, 8, 2, 87-105.

[126] Madanes, C. (2013). The 14 habits of highly miserable people. Retrieved November 2013 from
http://www.alternet.org/personal-health/14-habits-highly-miserable-people

[127] Reported in Yapko, M. D. (2003). *Trancework: An Introduction to the Practice of Clinical Hypnosis*. New York: Brunner-Routledge.   Kroger used hypnosis rather than chemical anaesthesia with many of his surgical patients.

[128] Milton Erickson was an outstanding American psychiatrist and hypnotherapist whose work with families and individuals working through problem relationships has been much studied. Erickson could induce a sort of

hypnotic suggestibility with one or two seemingly innocuous sentences or a handshake. A significant branch of NLP therapeutic work is rooted in Erickson's research and approach.

[129] http://www.silvamindbodyhealing.com/ When I checked in November, 2013, they offered a series of free lessons to get you started, and if try that and find it useful, you can spend money to get the rest of the programme.

[130] Modi also identifies what appear to be spiritual "attachments" (both well-meaning and malignant) causing dis-ease in her thought-provoking book. Modi, S. (1997). *Remarkable Healings: A Psychiatrist Discovers Unsuspected Roots of Mental and Physical Illness.* Charlottesville, Virginia, USA: Hampton Roads Publishing Company.

[131] Cahn, B. R., Delorme, A. & Polich, J. (2010). Occipital gamma activation during Vipassana meditation. *Cognitive Proces*sing, 11(1): 39-56. Retrieved from http://www.ncbi.nlm.nih.gov/pmc/articles/PMC2812711/

[132] This and a great deal more can be found in the excellent book *The Way of Qigong* by Kenneth S. Cohen, ©1997, New York: Ballantine Books. My copy is well-thumbed and dog-earred.

[133] Zhang, Z. J., Chen, H. Y., Yip, K., & Wong, V. T. (2009). The effectiveness and safety of acupuncture therapy in depressive disorders: Systemic review and meta-analysis. *Journal of Affective Disorders*, 24, 1, 9-21. Retrieved from http://www.jad-journal.com/article/S0165-0327(09)00311-5/abstract

[134] Rozman, D. (2013). Let your heart talk to your brain. Huffington Post. Retrieved November 2013 from http://www.huffingtonpost.com/heartmath-llc/heart-wisdom_b_2615857.html

[135] See Servan-Schreiver, D. (2003). *The Instinct to Heal: Curing Stress, Anxiety, and Depression Without Drugs and Without Talk Therapy*. Pennsylvania, USA: Rodale, and Salem, M. O. (2007) *The Heart, Mind, and Spirit*, retrieved from http://www.rcpsych.ac.uk/pdf/Heart,%20Mind%20and%

20Spirit%20%20Mohamed%20Salem.pdf

[136] Braden, G. (N.D.) Humanity at a cross-roads. from an interview with John Mann, retrieved November 2013 from http://www.greggbraden.com/press-and-media/humanity-at-a-crossroads

[137] Stim, E. (2010, updated 2013) Nerves and neurotransmitters in the heart. *Physician's Notebooks*. Retrieved November 2013 from http://physiciansnotebook.blogspot.co.nz/2011/03/nerves-and-neurotransmitters-in-heart.html

[138] Bowen, R. (2006). The Enteric Nervous System, retrieved from http://www.vivo.colostate.edu/hbooks/pathphys/digestion/basics/gi_nervous.html

[139] Sheldrake, R. (2009). *Morphic Resonance: The Nature of Formative Causation*. Toronto: Park Street Press.

[140] For a good summary of this research and its implications, see McTaggart, Lynne. (2008). The Field: The Quest for the Secret Force of the Universe. New York: Harper Collins.

[141] Laszlo, E. (2009). *The Akashic Experience*. Rochester, Vermont: Inner Traditions.

[142] Craig, G. (2010). *The EFT Manual*. Santa Rosa, CA: Energy Psychology Press. Also see Craig's short youtube video retrieved January 2014 from http://www.youtube.com/watch?v=VFKVVP8KXd4

[143] Dawson, K. & Allenby, S. (2010). *Matrix Reimprinting Using EFT*. Publisher: Hay House.

[144] Bays, B. (2012, revised edition). *The Journey: A Practical Guide to Healing Your Life and Setting Yourself Free*. New York: Atria Books.